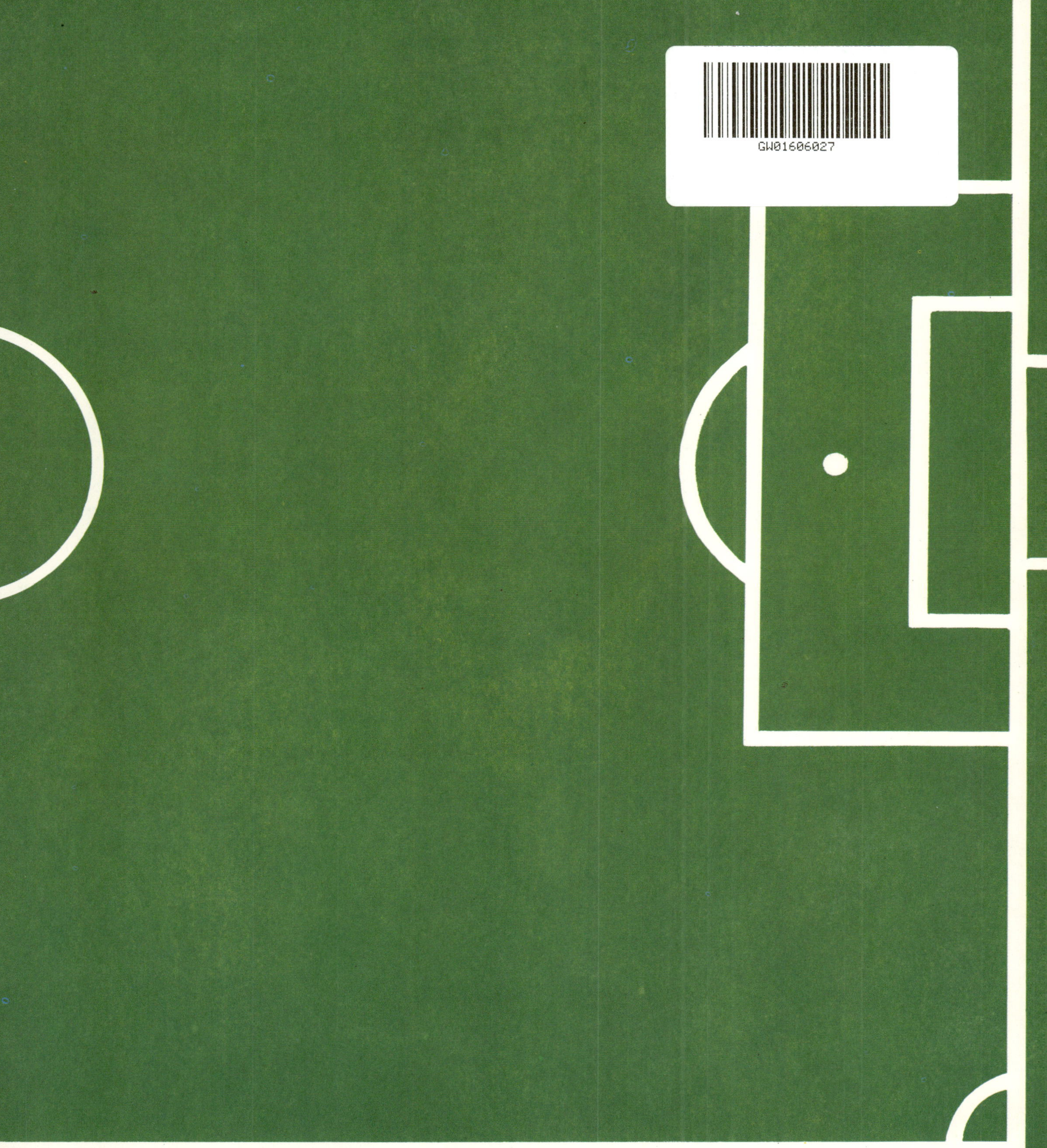

Although there is no substitute for practice on the field, with plastic or cardboard cut-out figures you can work out the movements described in the book on this 'table-top' pitch.

WHAT IT'S ALL ABOUT

A football game, whether it's a park scramble or a full-scale international, is a struggle between two sides for possession of the ball, with rapid switches from defence to attack and attack to defence as the ball is lost or won. Possession is the key to winning, for without the ball no goals can be scored. The team that wins possession starts the attacking movement, putting their opponents on the defensive and forcing them to challenge for the ball. When they lose possession, the roles are reversed: the attackers become the defenders, and the defenders take over as attackers.

For the *attackers* the *middle* of the field is a vital area in which to keep possession, as it is here that most attacks start to build up. Once they have forced their way into the last third of the field of play however, the attackers must be prepared to take a chance or two if they want to score, even at the risk of losing the ball.

For the *defenders* the one place where no risks can be taken is *the area in front of the goal*. Here they must play for safety.

To be a good team player you need to have mastery over the basic skills and a good knowledge of the rules of the game because your skills have to be applied within limits imposed by the rules.

Whether your team is attacking or defending you must be 'in the game' the whole time. When possession is lost the *whole* team is concerned with defence, and when the ball is regained *every* player has a part to play in the attack. Football is a *team* game.

Illustrations by 'Prof'
Diagrams by C. Rose

First published in 1972
Second impression 1973
Published by William Collins Sons and Co Ltd
Glasgow and London

ISBN 0 00 103312 3
Printed in Tenerife (Spain) by Litografia
A. Romero, S.A.

PLAY BETTER SOCCER

all in colour

CONTENTS

by Tom Saunders

COLLINS · GLASGOW AND LONDON

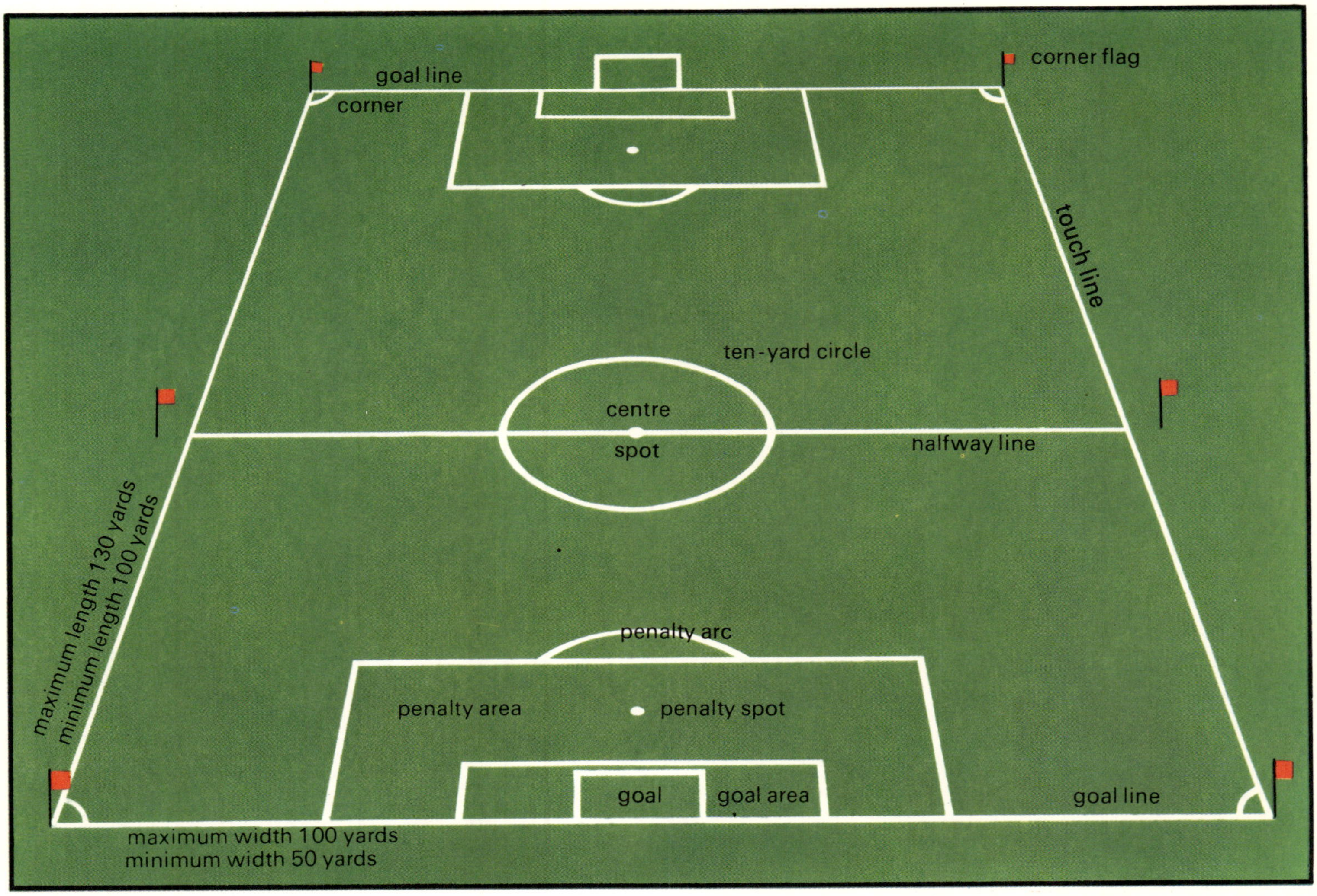

corner flag
goal line
corner
touch line
ten-yard circle
centre
spot
halfway line
maximum length 130 yards
minimum length 100 yards
penalty arc
penalty area
penalty spot
goal
goal area
goal line
maximum width 100 yards
minimum width 50 yards

The field of play

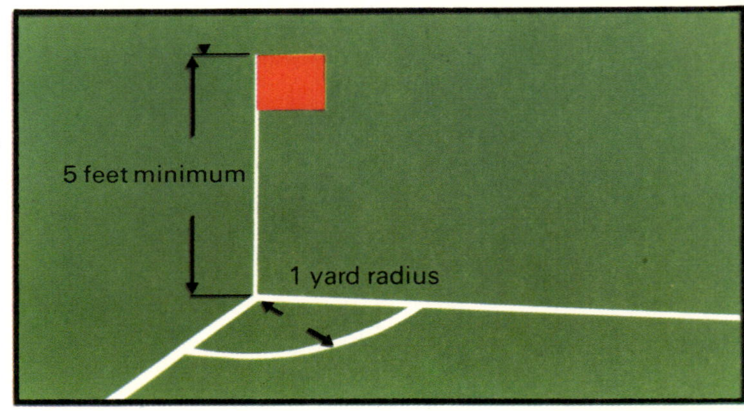

The rules of the game allow the dimensions of a football pitch to vary between certain maximum and minimum sizes, provided the length of the pitch is greater than its width. The maximum and minimum sizes allowed are shown on the diagram above. But whatever the length or width of a particular pitch, the distances of markings *inside* the pitch remain the same. For example, whether a pitch is marked out to the maximum or minimum dimensions allowed, the goal area is always a rectangle measuring 20 yards long by 6 yards wide, the centre circle always has a radius of ten yards, the penalty spot is always 12 yards from the centre of the goal-line, and so on.

All pitch markings should be clear and not more than 5 inches wide.

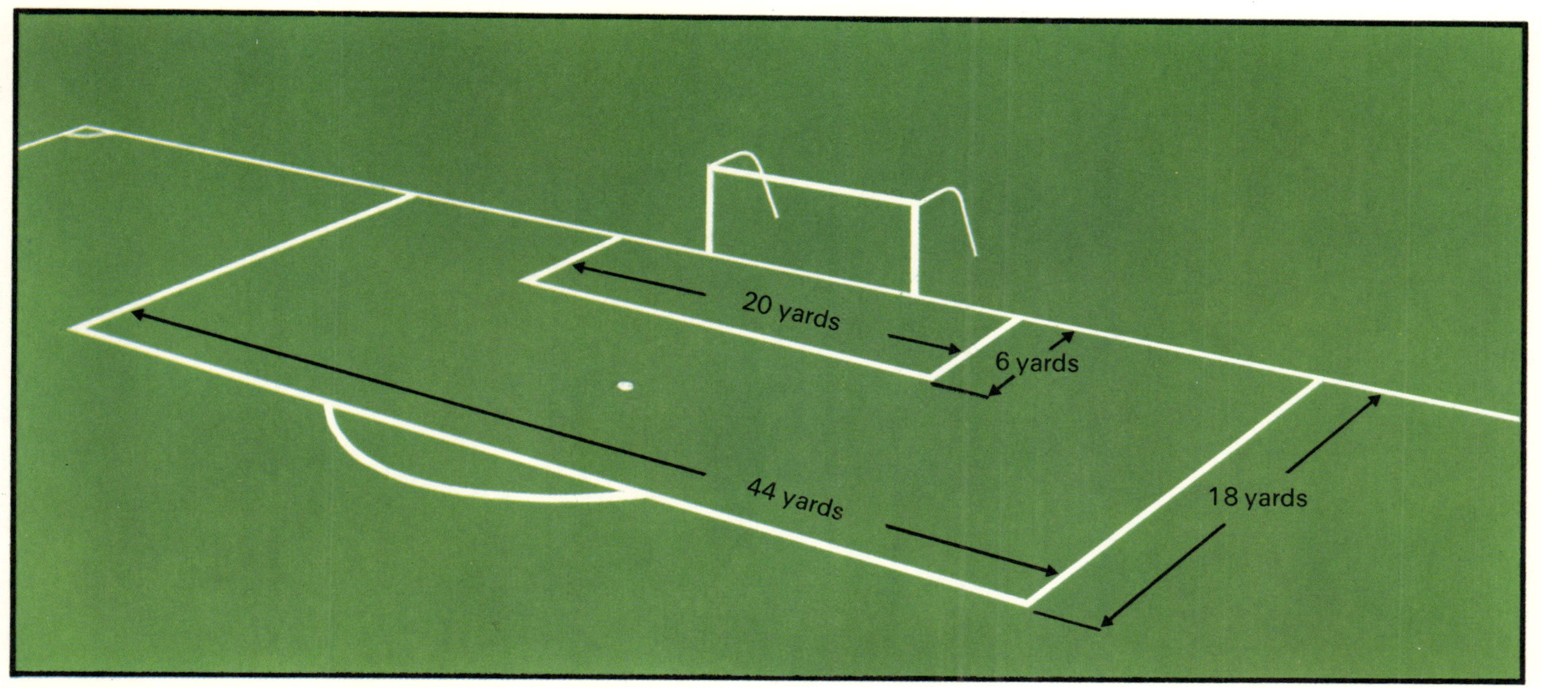

The penalty and goal areas:
The *penalty area* is a rectangle measuring 44 yards long by 18 yards wide. If any member of the defending side commits a penal offence inside this area a penalty kick is awarded to the attacker. The penalty offences are listed on page 48.) It is also the area in which the goalkeeper is allowed to handle the ball.

The *goal area* is a rectangle 20 yards long by 6 yards wide. This is the area in which the goalkeeper can be charged only if he is in possession of the ball, and the area inside which the ball must lie for a goal kick.

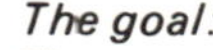

The goal:
The posts must be upright and equidistant from the corner flags. Measured from *inside* the posts and from the underside of the cross-bar the goal is 8 yards wide and 8 feet high. Posts and crossbar must be the same width and not more than 5 inches wide, and the goal-line must be the same width as the posts.

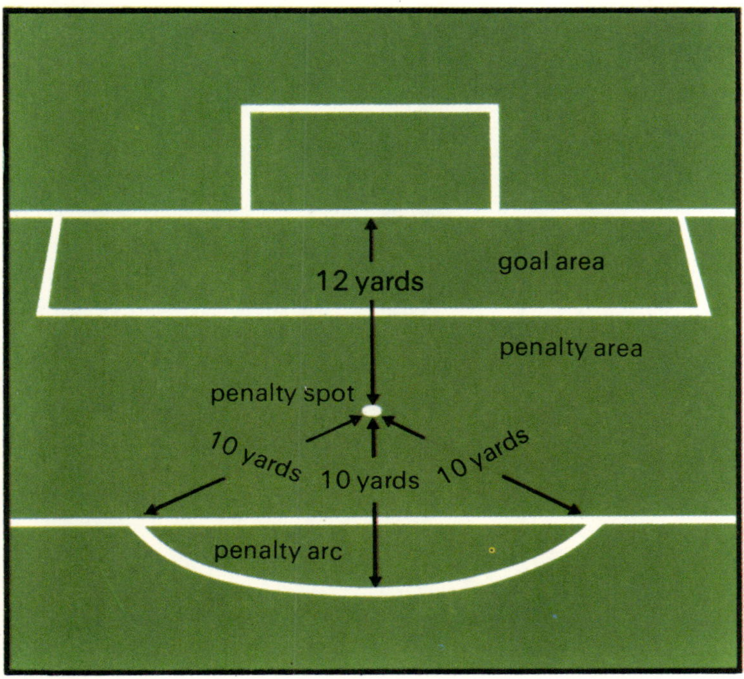

The penalty spot and penalty arc:
The point from which a place kick is taken when a penalty kick is given. It lies 12 yards from the centre of the goal-line.

The penalty arc does *not* form part of the penalty area; it is at 10 yards radius from the penalty spot and simply indicates the area into which players may not move until the kick has been taken.

A team consists of not more than eleven players, one of whom is the goalkeeper. In match play the keeper must wear a jersey of a different colour from that of the rest of his team.

The ball

The ball must be spherical and its case made of leather or some other officially approved material. The standard size, weight and pressure laid down in the F.A. rules are:

circumference: minimum 27 inches, maximum 28 inches
weight: not more than 16 oz and not less than 14 oz at the start of play
pressure: equal to 15 lb per square inch at sea level.

The standard ball
circumference: 27 to 28 inches
weight: maximum 16oz, minimum 14oz
pressure: 15lb per square inch

The players

A team consists of not more than eleven players, one of whom is the goalkeeper. The number of substitutes allowed will depend on the conditions under which the match has been arranged, but in any event substitutes may not enter the field of play until the referee signals to indicate that he agrees for them to do so. And no player may substitute for or change places with the goalkeeper without first informing the referee.

The equipment

The rules of the game provide protection for the players by stipulating that no player shall go on to the field wearing anything dangerous to another player (e.g. rings, watches, other metal or hard objects).

Boots may be fitted with bars and studs in any combination the player chooses so long as they are made of leather, plastic, soft rubber, aluminium or something similar, and are of the type and size permitted. Studs must be round and not less than ½ inch in diameter. Bars must extend across the whole boot width and all corners must be rounded. Neither bars nor studs may be more than ¾ inch deep. The only metal allowed is the metal seating of screw-in type studs.

The goalkeeper shall be distinguished from the other players in his team by wearing a different coloured shirt or jersey.

Every player is responsible for making sure that his boots conform to F.A. regulations. Check for loose studs and sharp edges before each game.

The referee

Once the game has started the referee (assisted by two linesmen) controls the game and the players. His role is to enforce the laws with complete fairness to both sides and to decide on disputed points. He keeps a record of the game, is the official timekeeper, and allows extra time for taking a penalty or for injuries and other stoppages. He has the power to stop play if he considers a player is seriously injured, send off or caution a player guilty of misconduct, decide if the ball has to be changed during the course of the game, and forbid any unauthorised person to enter the field of play.

His decision is final but once play has restarted he cannot reverse that verdict.

The linesmen

The linesmen signal when the ball goes over the touch line or the goal-line, and indicate the point at which it went out of play. They signal goal kicks, corner kicks, ball out of play and throw-ins in the area allocated to them. In the event of a disputed point the referee may consult the linesman but it is the referee alone who makes the decision.

Once the game begins the referee is in sole control of both play and players. He alone makes decisions on disputed points and his verdict is final. A whistle, notebook and pencil, a watch, and a coin for tossing for choice of ends are his 'equipment'.

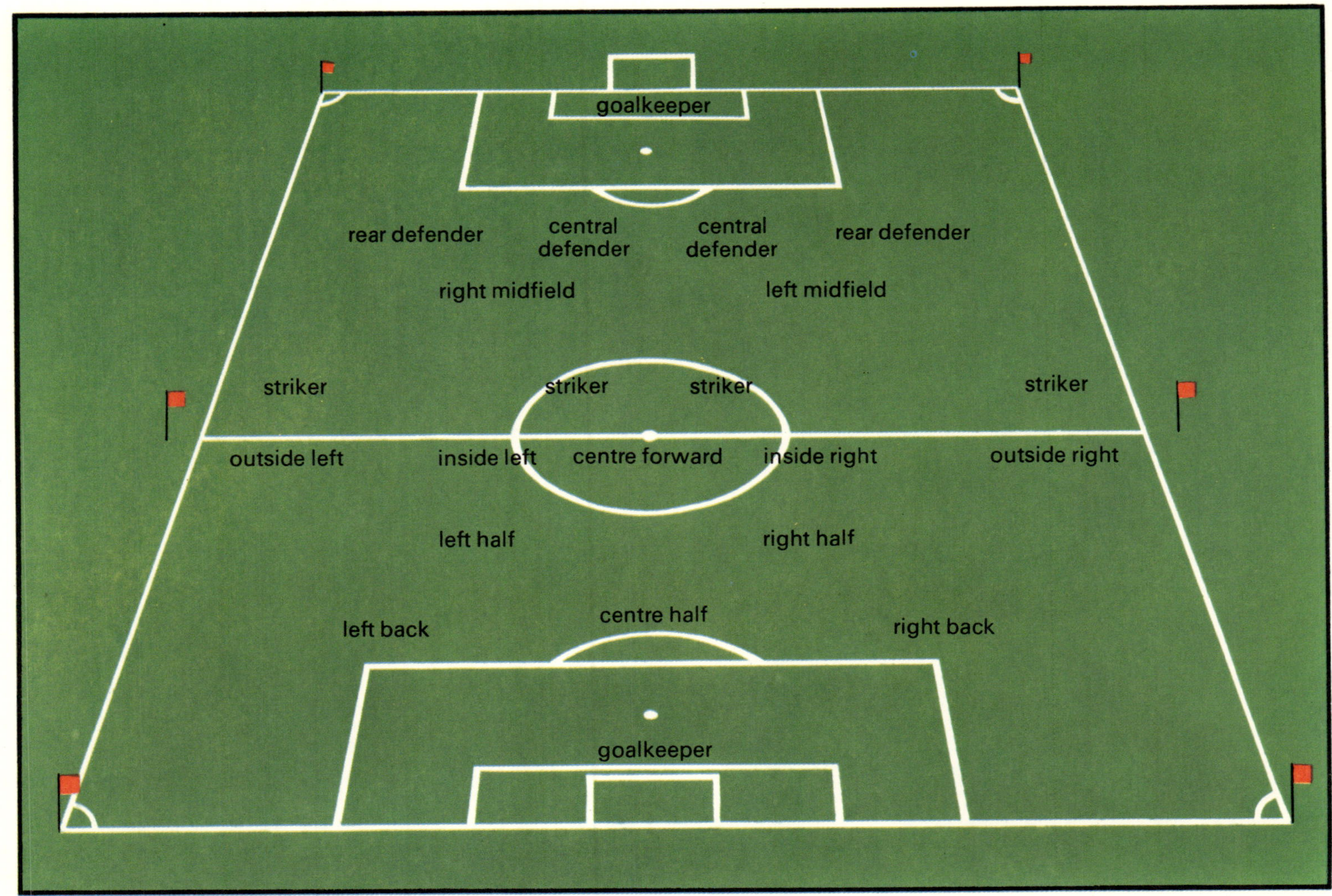

There is nothing in the laws of the game stipulating that the players shall play in certain positions. This diagram simply shows the approximate 'old style' and 'new style' line-up at kick-off. Once play begins the players adjust their positions freely in relation to the state of play.

Positions

In recent years far too much emphasis has been put on style of play and formations. At all levels of football players often think that it is the particular formation employed by the team that makes the difference between winning and losing. This is not so. The system must suit the needs of the individual abilities of the players in the team.

Drilling rigidly in 4–2–4, 4–3–3 and even in 4–4–2 is quite wrong for young players. The first essential is to develop an understanding of the basic principles of the game.

It is true that before the change in the offside rule in 1925 full-backs and half-backs concerned themselves with the business of defending while the forwards assumed responsibility for scoring goals. Times have changed: freedom of movement is an essential and accepted part of the game. It is not unusual in modern football for defenders to pop up quite regularly in the opponent's penalty area even to score a goal.

A good team that is well organised will move as a unit, with players constantly adjusting their positions in relation to the ball and the movements of their team mates. If great gaps appear between your defenders and midfield players and front men, you can be sure that these will be exploited by your opponents and will often result in a lot of chasing after the ball with little actual ball possession. When a defender moves forward to link up with the attack, the other defenders must be prepared to adjust their positions to balance his movement if the team loses possession and the attack breaks down.

One of the main differences between good and bad teams is the speed at which they move while remaining closely linked both in attack and defence. It is of the greatest importance that when in possession the whole team must think positively and when the ball is lost the whole team must act as defenders. Neither numbers on your players' shirts nor the system being employed by the team will make it successful. What *will* in the end make you a better player, well able to fit into *any* system or style of play, is an understanding of the basic principles of the game, together with a willingness to work hard for the team when you are not actually in possession of the ball.

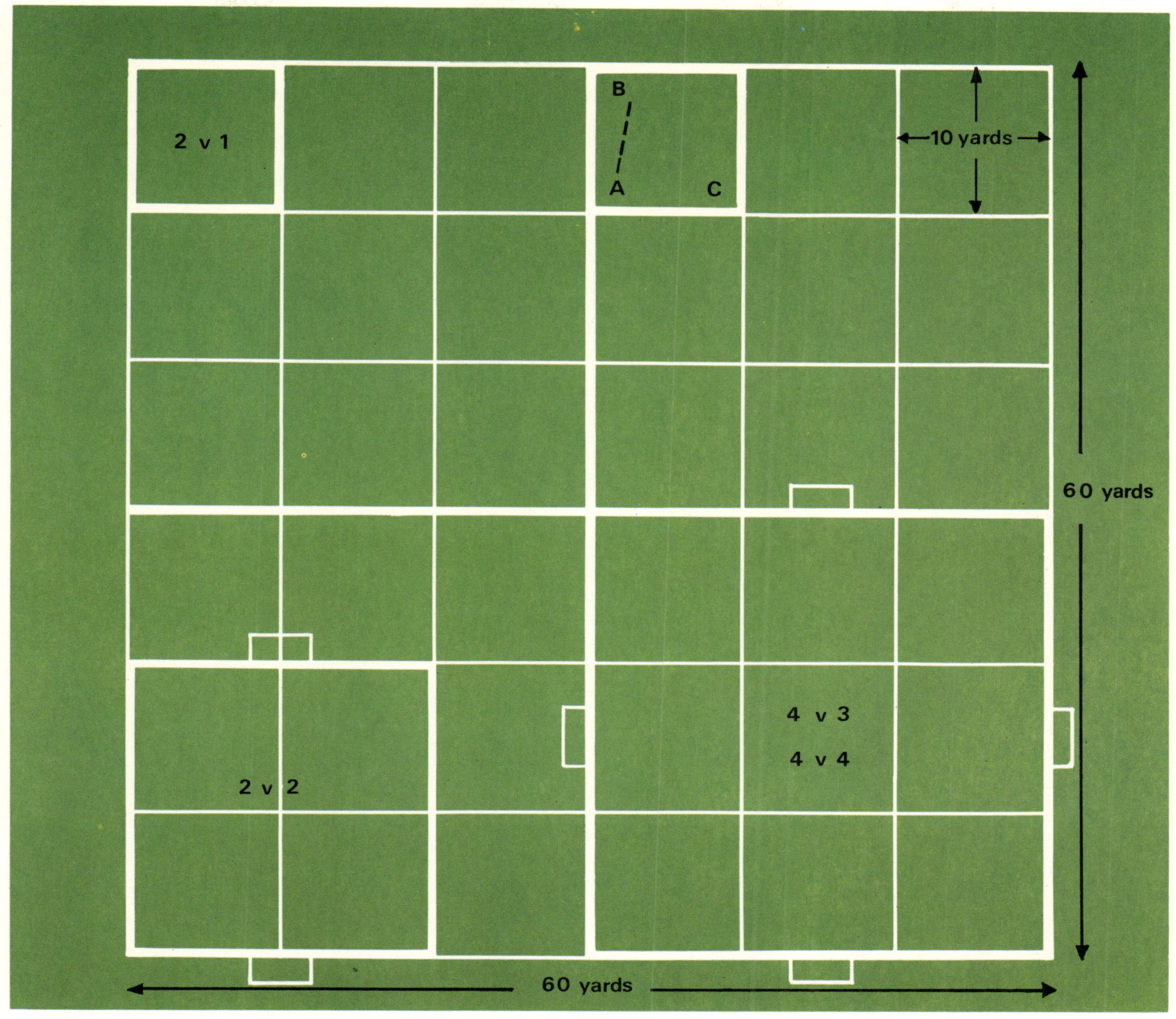

Using a training grid

Small-sided team games provide the best possible environment in which young players can experiment and improve their performance in the real game. The coaching grid, as it is often called, is a useful way of using a small area to the best advantage. The grid can be as small or as large as you wish to make it and is usually marked out in squares each measuring 10 yards long by 10 yards wide. The great advantage is that the squares can be joined together to form other areas of different sizes and shapes.

The diagram shows an area 60 yards long by 60 yards wide divided into 10-yard squares. The heavier lines show how the area can be split up to make playing areas of different sizes.

The game of football is a constant struggle between two teams who are very much concerned with the problems of time and space. The lower the skill of the individual player the more time and space he needs to execute the basic moves.

The training grid can be used in a variety of ways to enable realistic practice situations to take place:

1. Three players work in one square with two playing against one trying to make as many consecutive passes as possible without the opponent kicking the ball out of the square or intercepting it. Each player should take a turn at intercepting.

2. Good use can be made of the corners for simple technique practices. *A* plays the ball to *B* whilst *C* the opponent cannot move to prevent *A* and *B* combining to make consecutive passes until the ball has been played by *B*. This gives *B* time to control the ball before *C* makes his challenge.

Joining 4 squares together provides an ideal area to play 2 v. 2 or 2 v. 3. To give the practice realism and a sense of direction it is important to have a goal at each end of the pitch. It is also possible to split the area up, making 4 pitches 30 yards × 30 yards.

When the keeper comes out to take a high ball the rear defenders must quickly cover the exposed goal mouth against attack whenever they are able to do so.

Rear defenders

The way in which full backs play (or rear flank defenders as they are now sometimes called) has changed considerably in recent years. Full backs were looked upon as strong aggressive players with a powerful kick and fairly limited ball-playing skill. Today they must be as quick in movement and thought as any other player in the team, relying on intercepting and tackling in their challenge for the ball.

They are concerned with two main themes of defensive play:

(1) Man to man marking.
(2) Zone defence (i.e. marking space).

As you will see in the diagram opposite, in man-to-man marking each defender marks an opponent and tracks him wherever he goes, preventing him from receiving a pass or dispossessing him if he does. Players who are not concerned with any direct threat to the goal are also being marked. Defending players are also often drawn into a straight line position which means that when the ball is played past one the other defenders are also taken out of the game.

In zone defence, defenders instead of marking an individual player cover specific areas of the field and deal with any player who moves into their particular zone. In the diagram opposite the left back C has moved to challenge the outside right who is in possession of the ball whilst the left centre back moves to cover. In the event of C being beaten by the outside right the left centre back will then make his challenge and at the same time the other two defenders will move into good covering positions. If the outside right plays the ball back to his colleague B the left centre back will make a quick challenge for the ball whilst the other defenders adjust their positions to give cover.

If the threat to the goal is made from the other side of the field the defensive line will be angled in the opposite direction.

The nearer attackers get to your goal the more closely they must be marked.

A defender who finds that he has been beaten by the attacker should follow the line of retreat that will give maximum protection to the goal. If he is beaten out on the wing, he will retreat towards the near post. If he is beaten in midfield, he will take his line on the centre of the goal mouth.

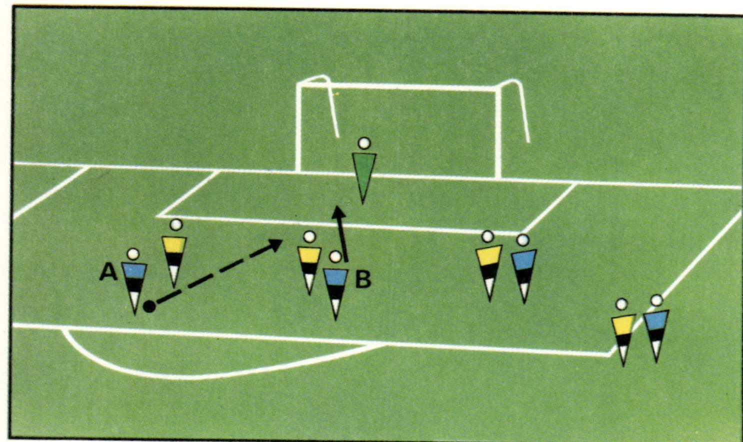

Man-to-man marking: each player has a set opponent to mark. So, in this diagram when attacker B moves to take the pass from A, his marker will move with him.

Zone defence: each defender has a certain area of the field to cover. So, in this diagram defender C marks both A and B who are both in his zone. When A passes the ball to B, C moves to mark and tackle.

When caught in possession of the ball facing his own goal and challenged for it, rear defender A plays it quickly and simply by passing to keeper B. Because he has a clearer view of the oncoming players, the keeper will have moved in anticipation of the pass. The rear defender then moves into a wide position, ready to receive a pass and start a fresh attacking movement downfield to C.

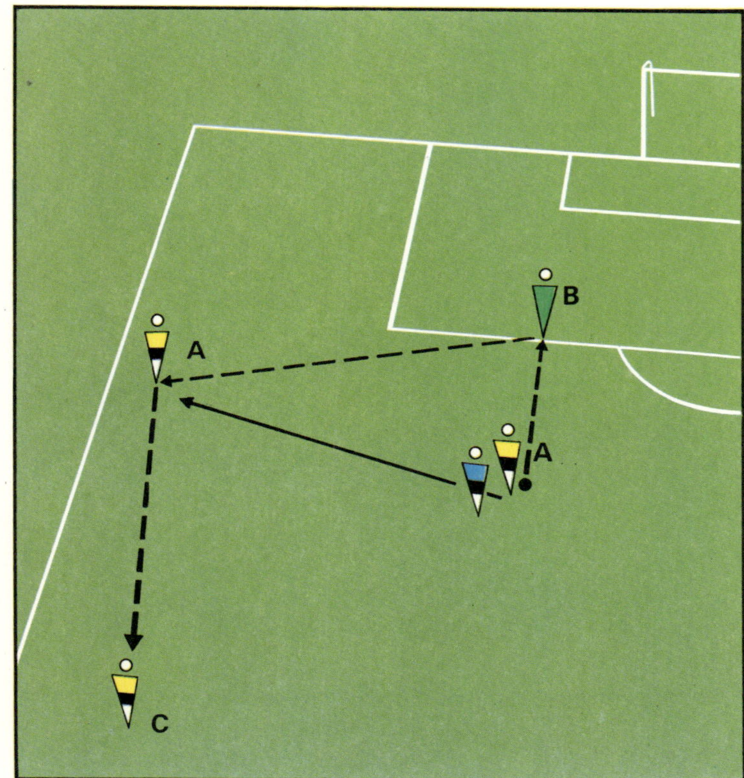

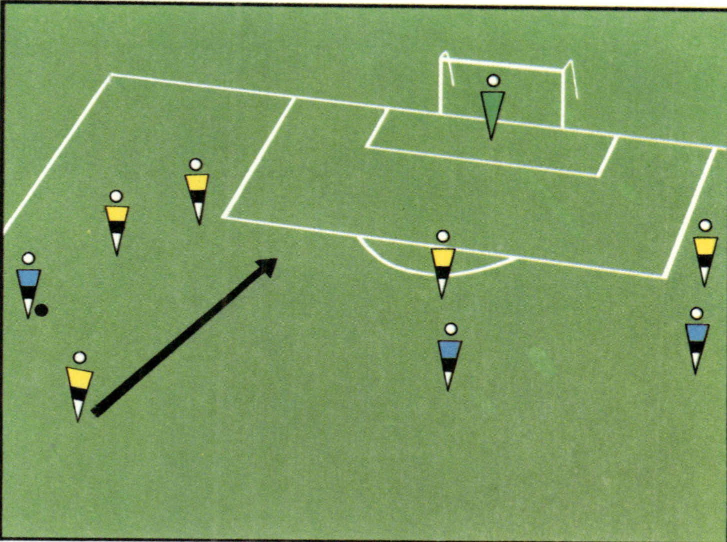

Line of retreat: when beaten by an opponent the rear defender must recover quickly to defend the vital space in front of the goal. If beaten out on the wing, take a line on the near post. Your team-mates may delay the attacker to give you time to get back.

If you are beaten in the middle of the field, take a central line of retreat.

Balancing the defence: each defender must adjust his position in relation to the rest. He must be ready to fall back or move forward as the state of play demands. The diagram shows how the right full back falls back to balance the defence line as the ball beats the defenders on the other side of the field.

Central defenders

A long high cross into the penalty area is a favourite method of attack against a well-organised defence. The central defenders must therefore become masters of the ball in the air, expert in jumping to head the ball away.

Ideally the ball should be headed towards a team mate but if the situation makes this impossible the defender must head for distance with as much height as possible to get the ball away from the danger area.

Quick and certain control of the ball is essential. Move quickly when danger threatens and play the ball early There is no time here for the clever player who wants to fiddle about with the ball.

Good clear kicking with both feet is one of the main skill requirements for a central defender. He must often kick the ball clear from the danger area when under considerable pressure and he must make contact with the ball before it touches the ground. The defender who allows the ball to bounce in front of him is asking for trouble.

Tackling and intercepting are both very important aspects of defensive play. Knowing when to tackle is vital. The defender in a 2 v. 1 situation who hustles in straight away is simply selling himself. If he delays his challenge too long he will also be at a disadvantage. When he cannot gain outright possession the clever defender learns how to delay the progress of attackers in order to gain time while the other defenders take up covering positions.

Try to force the attacking players to play the ball in front of you rather than past you. If you can do this you are part of the way to becoming a good defender.

Once a central defender has intercepted the ball he is often in a very good position to start up a quick attack by making a good long accurate kick either straight to one of his own players or into a space behind the opposing defenders ready for his team mates to pick up.

To turn a defensive position into a good attacking one in this way he needs to be quick to calculate the possible advantages of the quick, long clearance.

A central defender has to be master of the high ball in the air. Learn to time your jump and watch the ball on to your forehead. Head for distance if you are under pressure.

Turning defence into a good attacking position by using the lofted drive to make an accurate long pass upfield. The main disadvantage is that the longer the pass the greater the chance of interception. In this particular situation as the defender is under no particular pressure he may have other options.

Long clearance kick: there will be many situations in which you will not have time to control the ball: use the volley to get it away from the danger area.

The midfield men

Practise running with your head up. You cannot make accurate passes if you cannot see.

"The team that controls the middle of the field wins the match". There is a great deal of truth in this statement. Midfield players are the engine room of the team, constantly linking the defence with the attack.

Great demands are made on the players' fitness and stamina and if you are really coping you must have a high workrate and never be very far away from the ball.

A player in this position will need to be skilful in ball control, well balanced and with the ability to turn quickly when in possession of the ball. At the same time he must be an expert in judging *how, when* and *where* to pass. Accuracy in passing is a vital skill requirement.

Positional play is not rigid but he must be constantly responding to other players around him in order to help when they are in possession of the ball, providing good passing angles.

Having played the ball forward he must be quick to move in support of front players who are often tightly marked and are not able to turn without losing possession. The best move for his colleague is to lay the ball off into the path of the oncoming midfield player who can shoot for goal.

The midfield player has definite defensive responsibilities and when possession of the ball is lost his first job must be to get goal side of the ball. He will often win the ball by means of intelligent interception, having assessed accurately where the ball is going to be played.

You must be constantly aiming to improve your work in midfield defence as well as scoring goals.

Learn to make good passing angles to help the player with the ball. In the top illustration the player on the right has forced his team-mate to give the ball away to his opponent. In the middle illustration he has made a slightly better angle but the ball is certain to be intercepted. In the bottom illustration a safe passing angle has been made.

The strikers

The striker is the taker of chances rather than the maker of chances. The object of the game is to score goals and in order to do this there must be a player in a shooting position with the ball at his feet.

It is worth considering for a moment how goals are scored. If you were to make a careful check you would notice that the majority of goals are scored as a direct result of defensive mistakes.

The striker must move into scoring positions ready to chase and fight for every ball. The position calls for courage as there will be plenty of physical contact. Very often the striker will be heavily outnumbered, particularly when he is running at opponents and is in possession of the ball. All too often you see players in forward positions who are not prepared to assume responsibility for shooting at goal but are looking instead for players to pass the ball to.

Shooting is the key to success. You must be prepared to shoot even though there will be times when you cannot even see the target, and the angle seems to be an impossible one. Goalkeepers are human and will make mistakes from time to time, so make sure you bring them into action as often as possible.

When a ball is driven hard and low into a crowded goalmouth it is often deflected, or it may well rebound from the goalposts. Perhaps the goalkeeper is unable to hold the ball. The ever-alert striker must be ready to pounce on any defensive mistakes, creating goals out of nothing.

One way to assess your worth as a striker is to have someone check on the number of shots you have at the goal in each game, and whether they are on target, but above all remember if you don't shoot you will not score goals.

Good follow through after the moment of contact is important. Use your arms to lend balance.

Even when defenders block the goal the striker must still shoot through the narrowest of gaps. Remember that the keeper may also be unsighted and at a disadvantage. Once you are in the penalty area with the ball at your feet the golden rule is *shoot!*

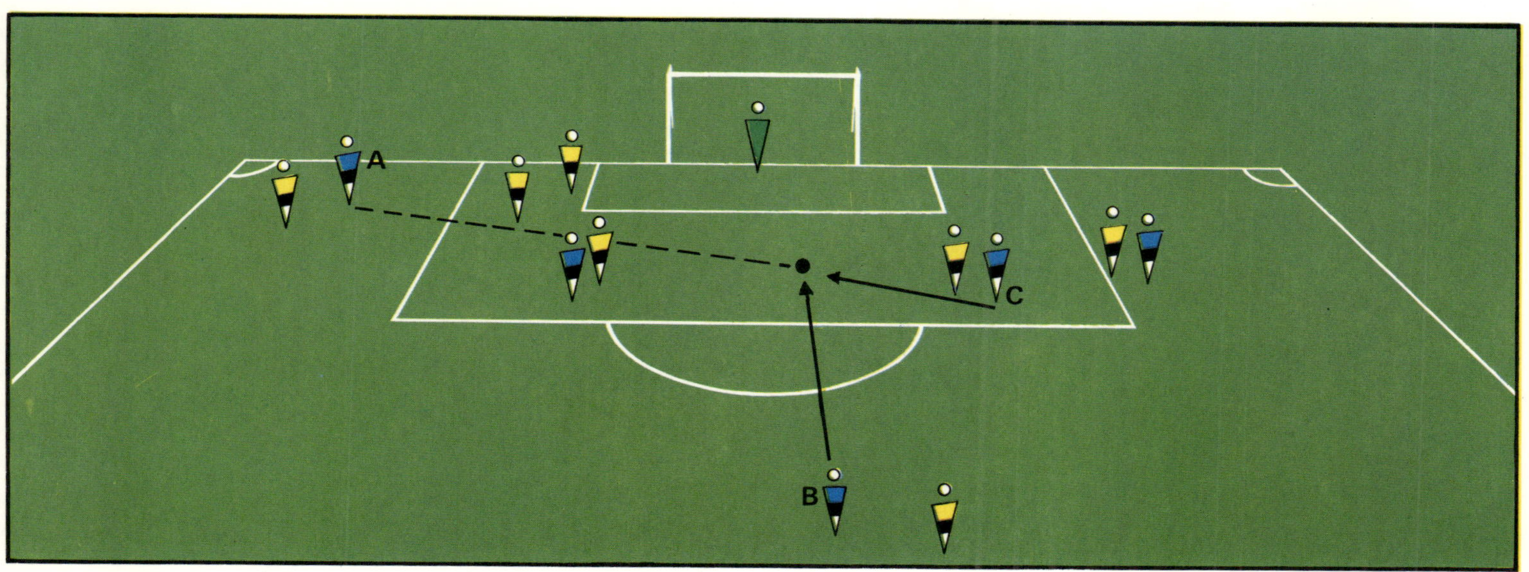

The striker must be quick to move in to take a shot at goal from cross passes made from either wing. All forward players must be prepared to move into space to anticipate the movement of the ball in order to get a shot at goal. In moves of this kind it is the striker's speed that beats the defenders.

It is usually the striker who takes corner kicks.

The overhead ball: keep eyes glued on the flight path of the ball. Spread your fingers behind it to reduce the danger of it slipping through.

The chest-high ball: body well behind the ball. Catch with both hands and control by pulling it in close to your chest. Concentrate on the ball and not the players challenging for it.

The ground ball: one knee bent, palms upwards to take the ball in to the pit of the stomach. If the ball slips through your hands, it comes up against foot and thigh.

The keeper

This is the one really specialised position in the team and needs a player who is alert, agile and—above all—able to concentrate. The keeper may have to remain out of the game for long periods and then suddenly be called upon to win the match with an outstanding save when everything looks set for a certain goal. He also needs enough courage to go down at the feet of an oncoming forward and risk heavy body contact. But there is more to playing keeper than sheer toughness. Watch the cat-like movements of the top-class keepers for lessons in alertness and technique.

HANDLING

As a rule all high centred balls inside the goal area should be left for the keeper to deal with because he is the only player allowed to handle the ball (and only inside the penalty area). This gives him a great advantage over other contenders for the ball, and he must learn to make full use of it. One of his best assets will be a safe pair of hands.

TWO HANDS ARE BETTER THAN ONE

Avoid knocking the ball down and never use one hand if you can get two to the ball. Tipping the ball over the bar or round the side of the post looks spectacular but both are often unnecessary tactics and are always desperation moves. Both end in a corner to the other side's advantage. Even punching clear is second best to clean catching. If you do find yourself with no option but to punch clear in an emergency, use both fists to give a bigger (and safer) punching surface. Use the flat part of the fist between knuckles and the first finger joints, punching high and for distance.

CLEARING

The keeper is allowed to take *not more than 4 steps* while holding, bouncing or throwing the ball in the air and catching it again. The penalty for taking more than 4 steps is an indirect free kick to the other side.

Having gained possession, most keepers clear to an unmarked team mate with a *short accurate throw* or by *rolling* the ball straight to his feet. The alternatives are a *long, overarm throw* (useful when the keeper is surrounded, or a *long drop-kick* upfield. Both take longer to reach their man than a short throw, and this gives the opposition time to recover. And neither the long throw nor the long drop-kick achieve very much if they simply land at the feet of a waiting opponent.

When not directly involved in the play the keeper normally stands on the six-yard line, ready to move in relation to the ball.

Corner kick: the keeper must be on his toes, able to see both the kicker and the ball. He must watch for the outswinger (dash line) and the inswinger (dots and dashes in the diagram). A is taking the kick with his right foot, and B is taking his outswinger with his left foot.

Penalty kick: the keeper must stand on his goal line between the posts and without moving his feet until the ball is kicked. Most keepers stand crouched in the middle of the goal mouth ready to make a spring for the ball in whatever direction it comes.

Having gained possession of the ball the goalkeeper is in a position to set up an attacking movement. In order to do this well he must be able to kick or throw with great accuracy. There is little merit in kicking a long high ball if this means giving it away to the defending players. On the other hand it may well be that you have a big forward who is good in the air, and this could mean that a defensive position could be transformed into an attacking one with a single kick.

Most keepers throw the ball, and a pass can be made by rolling the ball underarm or throwing it the same way as a cricket ball. The short accurate throw is best.

Narrow the angle of shooting for an attacker by coming forward and giving him a smaller target area. By moving slightly off centre at the same time you will tempt him to aim for the slightly wider target and can almost anticipate his shot.

Controlling the ball

The rules allow the players to control the ball with any part of their body except arms and hands. The illustrations show the different ways of making effective use of this rule.

The secret of control is to move fast towards the ball and get as close to it as you can. Decide quickly which part of your body you are going to use and then—before the ball makes contact with it—relax the surface. Then, just as the ball makes contact with chest, foot or thigh, withdraw very slightly and smoothly, moving with the ball, just enough to absorb the impact and send the ball to the ground close to your feet. Then move on to it fast before your opponents have a chance to rob you of it.

Until you learn to 'give' with the ball, it will bounce maddeningly away from you, out of control and giving the other side a good chance of regaining possession.

Get two other players to practise with you as follows: Player 1 serves the ball to Player 2 with varying types of service (in the air and on the ground). Player 2 has to control the ball while resisting the challenge of Player 3. It will usually be necessary for Player 2 to shield the ball with his body to avoid losing possession.

Controlling with the chest

Bring the ball down with the inside of the foot.

Controlling with the thigh.

Controlling with the outside of the foot.

Controlling with the inside of the foot.

Dribbling

Running with the ball and dribbling it tantalisingly past opponents is one of the satisfactions of a good player. There is no finer sight in soccer than a skilful forward running straight at the defenders while in full control of the ball, just taunting them to come and try to take it from him. It's great entertainment for the spectators and utter confusion for the defenders.

The forward player who is not prepared to take on defenders when he is near to the goal is not worth his place in the side.

The main problem for most players is making the right decision: when to dribble and when to pass. It is a decision of great importance because in certain parts of the field he cannot afford to lose possession of the ball. Some sorry sights have been seen when full backs have decided to try to *dribble* the ball out of their own penalty area instead of passing.

Running with the ball: play the ball with the outside of the controlling foot each time it comes forward in its stride.

In a 2 v. 1 situation watch the challengers as well as the ball.

When you are running with the ball you may have to screen it from an opponent either by putting your body between him and the ball or by taking the ball away from the side on which he is making his approach, as shown here.

Beating your man

Dribbling will, of course, immediately bring the defence chasing to stop the threat to their goal. So the skilful dribbler has to learn the art of deceiving his opponents with the many tricks of his trade: swerving, lightning changes of pace and direction, feinting, side-stepping, shifting his body weight from one foot to the other, looking suddenly away while continuing to run straight on with the ball, and showing the ball to his opponent only to drag it away with the side of his foot at the last moment as the defender comes lungeing in.

All these are the tricks and feints to shake the defence off. But before you can weave and feint with the smoothness of the professionals you will need to experiment and practise off the field until you are foot perfect.

Start by playing 1-against-1 in a small space, playing the ball with the outside of the controlling foot each time you take a forward stride. Keep the ball within playing distance all the time, tempting your opponent to come in and make his challenge when he is likely to be off balance and thereby giving you the best chance of beating him.

Most players make a point of mastering one or two particular tricks to the point of perfection to pull out of the bag at a moment's notice when the occasion demands it.

Deceiving your opponent: 1. Move to the left as if to play the ball with the inside of your right foot. 2. Step over the ball with your right foot, at the same time playing it with the outside of your foot to the side of the oncoming defender. 3. While he is recovering, play the ball past him with your *right* foot.

Stopping the ball quickly: you can often evade a tackle by stopping the ball quickly with the sole of your foot and dragging it back and moving in another direction.

Front players in modern football will frequently find themselves outnumbered by defenders when they receive the ball, and with supporting players some distance away and unable to give quick support. In this sort of situation a striker must have the ability to move quickly to receive a pass, feinting to go one way while keeping his body between his opponent and the ball, then turning quickly to make sufficient space to face the defender. Having created this situation he must then attack the defender with the ball. The experienced defender will probably retreat, at the same time trying to jockey the attacker away from the danger zone or into a restricted space (*e.g.* near the touch line). It is therefore important for the attacker to increase the speed of his dribble while going directly at the defender in an effort to beat him.

It is good practice to make use of the training grid to learn the right technique of keeping the ball within comfortable playing distance and maintaining an even balance while running. At first each player has a ball with which to practise inside a small area. Then, when the technique has been mastered, progress to a 1 *v.* 1 situation—still keeping within a confined space (one of the 10-yard grid squares is ideal) and with the player in possession of the ball trying to get his opponent in an off-balance position by feinting to go one way then shifting his body weight quickly to the other foot and moving off in a different direction.

It is essential for all players to have some dribbling ability no matter what their particular position in the team. Try to practise in a realistic way new methods of deceiving your opponent. You will not always succeed but you must be prepared to work hard at this aspect of the game, for it can be rewarding.

The instep kick: aim for the goalkeeper and keep your shot low. Remember the following points:

Place the non-kicking foot alongside the ball
Knee of the kicking leg well over the ball
Ankle stretched back, with toe pushed down
Kick *through* the ball
Eye on the ball.

Kicking

Mastery of kicking is vital, because this is what the game is really all about. A poor kicker can do nothing to hide his weakness no matter how good he is in other departments of the game. So priority number one for all aspiring players is kicking. There is no short cut to perfection: progress comes only with working hard at it. And both feet must come in for equal treatment. A player with a 'right' foot and a 'wrong' foot can be a menace to his side. By the time he's shuffled a good pass from his 'wrong' foot to his 'right' foot a good shooting chance has probably been lost and his opponents will have had time to take up defensive positions to meet his threat. So aim to develop two 'right' feet.

A good striker will get great satisfaction in developing a good kicking technique, and a rear defender who can find the team mate furthest away from him with a long, *accurate* kick is an enormous asset to his side. Too many players have to take the easy option of the short ball simply because they are poor kickers.

VARIATIONS ON THE KICK

There is of course more than one way to kick a football; different situations require different techniques and different techniques will produce very different results. The illustrations on pages 30 and 31 show some of the variations.

The lofted drive, the flick, the push, the chip kick, the volley and the half volley all have their useful moments. Being able to execute them well and knowing when to use them is the mark of a player of class.

'BENDING THE BALL'

Putting swerve on the ball is another useful accomplishment. It is a shot that can cause many a goalkeeper to mishandle the ball and give away a goal. Have fun by striking the ball with your instep off centre. In shooting practice you will see that the ball will spin to left or right depending on which side you strike the ball

THE NON-KICKING FOOT

The most important thing to develop is probably the simplest but the most neglected: the correct position of your non-kicking foot. Unless it is correctly placed in relation to the ball you will never have complete control over the direction or the trajectory of the ball. If the non-kicking foot is ahead of the ball at the moment of kicking, the trajectory will be low—and mainly useless. If it is placed too far behind the ball when the kick is taken, the trajectory will be a soaring one, giving the opposition plenty of time to intercept the pass and opportunity.

The kicking foot position at the moment of impact in an instep kick: ankle flexed, instep flat and toe down.

Chip kick
Overhead kick
Instep kick
Volley
Half volley

The lofted drive: knee of kicking leg well behind the ball, non-kicking foot slightly to one side and just behind the ball, body leaning slightly back as the kicking foot comes forward.

Which kick?

THE CHIP KICK

This kick is made using the inside of the instep. The toe of the kicking foot is stabbed under the ball, making it rise steeply over a very short distance.

This is a very useful way of getting the ball accurately to a team mate after clearing opponents who are in the way.

The stabbing action underneath the ball has to be done quickly and is fairly easily performed as the ball is gently rolling towards you.

THE INSTEP KICK

The important thing is to have the non-kicking foot alongside the ball and the kicking knee over the ball. Keep your eye on the ball as you make contact and use your arms to help with balance. When contact is made the ball will keep low.

THE VOLLEY

This kick is performed when contact is made with any part of the foot when the ball is in the air. The distance the ball travels will depend largely on the length of the swing made by the kicking leg and the height of the ball. The lower the ball the greater the swing.

THE HALF VOLLEY

This kick is made as the ball touches the ground and can be made with any part of the foot.

THE LOFTED DRIVE

Use the inside of the instep, the non-kicking foot slightly to one side of the ball and just behind it. Lean slightly backwards as you bring your kicking leg forward and make sure there is a good follow through.

Shooting

The ability to put the ball into the back of the net is the main skill requirement of the striker. This involves more than just kicking or heading the ball correctly. It requires great confidence and courage, good control and concentration, and above all the will to overcome frustration by believing that your next attempt at goal will be successful.

It is essential to be alert inside the penalty area and have a keen sense of anticipation of what may happen to the ball. A misheaded clearance, an awkward bounce, a deflection, an error of judgment on the part of a defender under pressure must be looked for as possibilities before they actually occur. The player who is able to anticipate these situations and is hungry for goals is bound to be successful.

Rarely will you be given the opportunity of a long run with the ball for a shot at goal. Your opportunities will occur mainly in a crowded penalty area, giving you little time and space in which to make contact with the ball.

The ability to turn quickly and shoot all in one movement is essential. This requires being aware of your position in relation to the goal at all times even though you may have your back to the target.

Young players presented with a scoring opportunity often make the mistake of trying to kick the ball too hard, with the result that it finishes in the crowd instead of the net.

Supreme confidence, courage and determination are all essential factors in the art of scoring. What a lift for your team if you score a great goal with a chance that has been made out of nothing!

Practise as often as you can—and in real situations—the art of shooting. And remember that the striker will almost always be tightly marked and there will be a need for quick control and shooting from different angles and heights. Practise coming off a defender when receiving a pass, creating for yourself just sufficient space to get a half turn and a shot at goal.

One of the many problems in football is the *ball watcher,* the player who just watches the ball and is quite prepared to let things happen rather than make them happen. The striker must be quick to follow the shot in, for often it will rebound from the goalkeeper or the woodwork and present a scoring opportunity that may appear to be simple but in fact is the result of the quick and alert player making the most of his chances.

Practise accurate shooting with both feet. Try to perfect the art of curling sharp shots into the bottom and top corners of the net.

If a defender blocks your path, pass the ball very quickly to any team-mate who has a clear sight of the goal.

Passing

Push pass.

Every player has played with the 'ball watchers'. If they are not in possession of the ball, they just don't play.

For many players, 'running off the ball' simply means sprinting smartly downfield in straight lines, leaving the player with the ball in splendid but useless isolation. What the ball watchers fail to understand is that it is the players *without* the ball who virtually dictate the course of play by the passing opportunities they create for their team mate with the ball.

THE PLAYER WITHOUT THE BALL

Passing depends largely on intelligent and unselfish running by team mates to support the player in possession. This involves moving in all directions, often to tempt defenders away from good defensive positions, but mostly to make good passing angles.

The player in possession may not always be in a position to see a team mate. It is therefore important for players to use their voices as well as their feet. You cannot play football successfully unless you exchange useful information with your team mates. There will always be situations when one player is better placed than another to decide the best course of action, particularly for the man with the ball.

Soccer is a game for *thinkers*. The how, when and where to run when *not* in possession of the ball are as important as knowing what to do once you are in possession.

Passing with the outside of the foot.

THE MAN IN POSSESSION

Now for the player with the ball. Sound advice to him is to play it simply and play it safe.

You cannot play the ball accurately if you can't *see*. So get your head up to judge the passing possibilities. Be aggressive in your passing by looking for the player furthest from you, and if the pass has a reasonable chance of success, *play it,* making sure you give it to your team mate at the right angle, the right height and the right speed for him to trap easily.

The better the standard of game you play in, the less time you will have for making decisions, and you will often have to decide where to play the ball even before it reaches you. The better the class of football, the more successful first time passes you will see, simply because the players involved are thinking ahead, anticipating their next move *before* they have to make it.

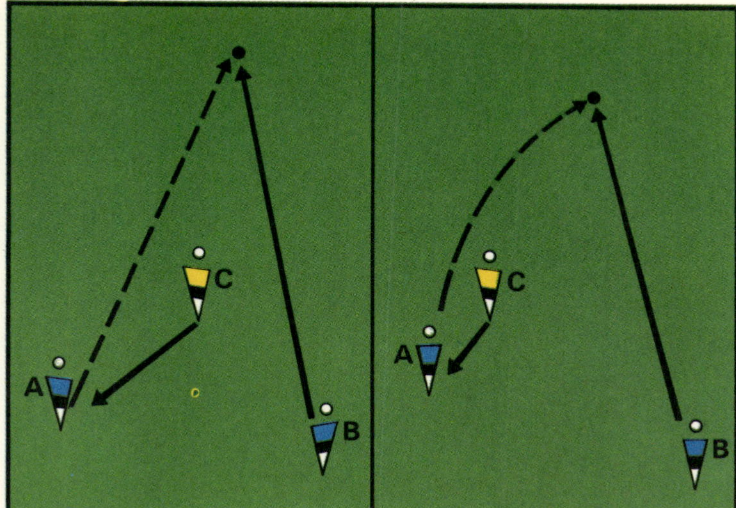

Far left: a simple forward pass.

Left: playing the ball behind the defender.

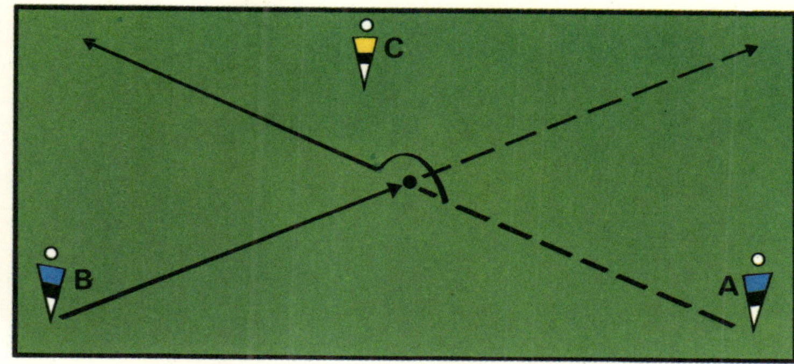

Scissors pass: player A is moving diagonally across field with the ball. C comes in to tackle. Player B runs diagonally across A's path. At the point where their paths cross A leaves the ball and continues his run to confuse C. B immediately picks up the ball as he continues in *his* run. The direction of the attack has been completely changed.

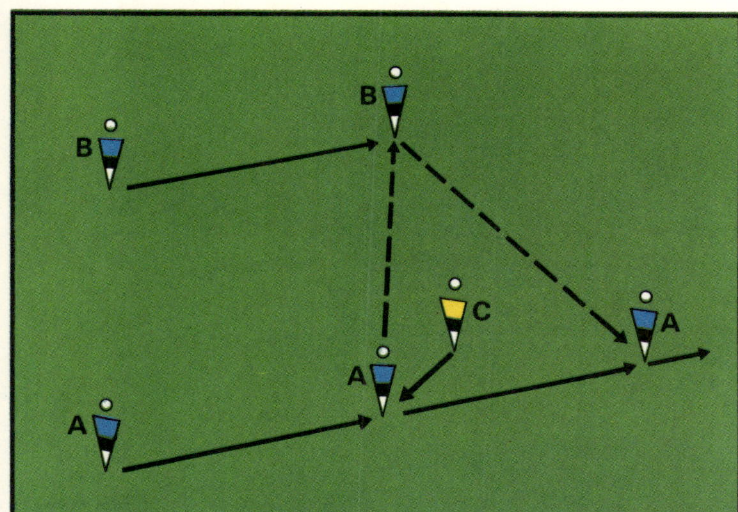

Wall pass: a player with the ball and a team mate running alongside must get past a single defender. Player A runs at the defender with the ball and before committing himself fully passes the ball to B, who acts as a wall, playing it behind the defender into the path of A who has sprinted past the defender.

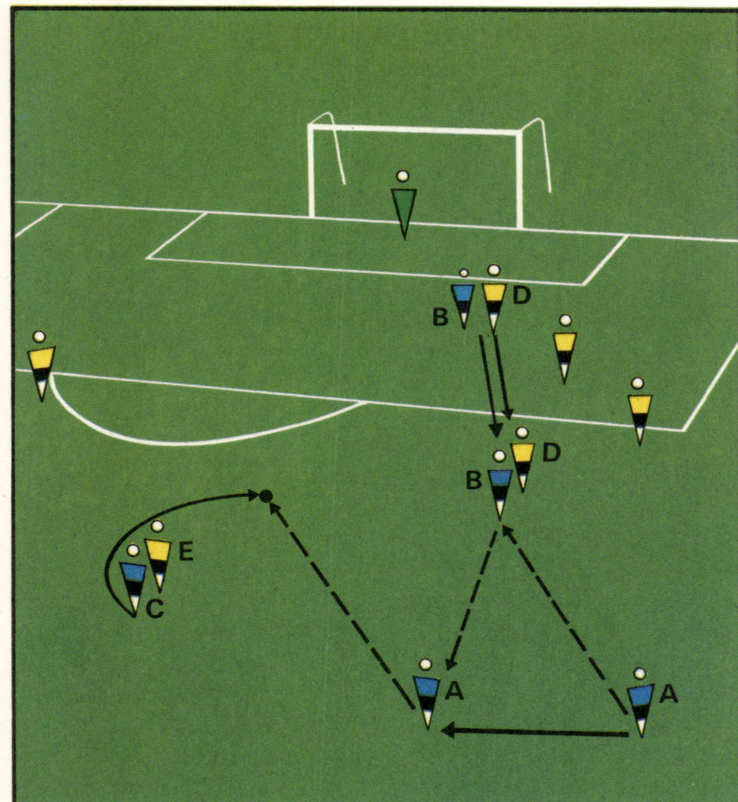

Setting up play and movement off the ball: attacker A has moved towards team mate B with the ball and the first pass is made to B's feet. The pass is set up to draw defender D out of position The second pass is returned to A who now plays the ball into space behind the defender marking C, who moves behind his marker and takes the ball in his stride for a shot at goal.

When to play to space and when to play to feet: player B has moved towards team mate A who plays the ball accurately to his feet so that he can play a first-time return angled back to A who has moved to a new position. Without delay A then plays the ball into the big space behind the defending players to enable C to move across on to the ball and exploit the new situation.

The block tackle: you must tackle with your whole body. Make your tackle as your opponent is about to play the ball. Strike the ball with the inside of your foot. This provides a larger surface.

Tackling

Most forwards play well as long as they have plenty of time and space. But they are not always so happy or so dangerous when they are strongly challenged before they have time to bring the ball under control. A defending player who manages to put in a couple of resounding tackles early in the game and win the ball is sure to have a good match as his opposite number will not only be thinking about what to do with the ball but also worrying about the tackle he knows will surely come.

Size and weight have little to do with successful tackling. The smallest player in the team can win the ball if he is a determined tackler. It's the player who half-heartedly goes through the motions of sticking out a leg that finishes with bruised shins and without the ball.

COMING OUT WITH THE BALL

Knowing *when* to tackle is every bit as important as knowing *how* to tackle. The player who lunges wildly and finishes up on the ground *without* the ball is serving his team badly. The good tackler is patient, waiting for the best moment and striking quickly when he sees that he has the best chance of *winning* the ball.

The best tackling practice is to play 2-v-2 in a small space with a goal at each end. In this situation you will be faced with the frequent body contact that is needed in learning the technique of tackling.

'Reading' the play is a very important aspect of defensive play as it enables a defender to close up quickly on an attacker just as he is about to control the ball. This is exactly the moment when the attacker is most vulnerable, for his attention will be divided between controlling the ball and the likely challenge by the defender. If the attacker should gain control and face the defender, the technique of jockeying should be used: here the defender angles his run when making his approach to invite the attacker to move in a certain direction, either away from the immediate danger area or into the line of defenders. If he takes the second course, then he should expect his team mates behind him to guide him by calling which way the attacker should be sent.

To develop the correct techniques of good defensive play it is best to play small-sided team games. These will improve your understanding of *how* and *when* to tackle in real situations.

To evade the tackle you may have to screen the ball from your opponent by putting your body between him and the ball.

Evading the tackle: pass the ball round the side of your opponent.

Evading the tackle: back heel the ball.

Evading the tackle: put the ball 'through the door' (between your opponent's legs).

Heading

Leading with the head is an unnatural movement and the first attempts can be painful. Being thumped on the wrong part of the head with a heavy ball can be discouraging even for the most enthusiastic player. A lightweight plastic ball is the best solution to the uncomfortable first efforts until you have mastered the technique of keeping your eye on the ball until just before making contact with the forehead.

A common heading fault is flicking at the ball with the side of the head. Real power in heading comes from a back-to-front movement that starts at the hips and ends with a kind of nodding down motion from the forehead.

RUN AND JUMP

The correct technique is not to wait for the ball but to run to meet it and jump for it. Timing the run is important because if you get there too early you will be right underneath the ball and unable to give it either power or direction. The timing of the *jump* is as important as the timing of the run. Use a single-footed take-off to get all the height that is needed.

While a tall player has an obvious natural advantage in heading, constant practice to get the timing of the run and jump perfect will overcome any lack of inches.

HEADING AS AN ATTACKING MEASURE

Heading can be used as an attacking as well as a defensive measure. A watchful forward lurking on the far side of the goal who matches the flight of the ball with a perfectly timed run and jump has a very good chance of putting the ball powerfully into the net out of the goalkeeper's reach.

Keep your eye on the ball and watch it until just before contact is made.

A cross pass headed quickly down into the bottom of the goal mouth often catches the keeper on the wrong side of the goal.

A striker often receives a high ball when he has his back to the goal. With a carefully timed run and jump to get the ball before the opposing defence he heads the ball down into the path of an oncoming team mate.

Small-sided team games

Throw-head-catch is a useful practice game for improving your heading technique.

Spending hours kicking a ball about may improve your mastery over it, but it will not necessarily make you a better player. Controlling the ball on an uneven pitch when an opponent is making a strong challenge for it presents very different problems.

The real test of a good player lies in the ability to recognise situations quickly when they occur in the game and then come up with the right actions. You can only develop this ability to 'read' situations by playing some kind of team game, and the best way to go about it is by playing small-sided team games on a small pitch with large goals.

It is not a bad idea to play a 'match' even if there is only a handful of players. Three players would mean 2 *v* 1, five players 3 *v* 2, seven players 4 *v* 3, and so on. The score will reach double figures but at least there will be plenty of scoring opportunities, which is what you need to learn to deal with.

The games can be varied to improve whichever of the basic skills you want to concentrate on. Here are a few suggestions:

Keep ball (to improve passing techniques). In addition to scoring in the usual way, if your team can make five consecutive passes without your opponents touching the ball, you score a goal.

Man-for-man marking. When your team loses possession of the ball everyone has a definite opponent to mark. When you win the ball, you are free to go where you want. This will help all players to realise that they have work to do both in attack and defence.

Two-touch. Each player may touch the ball only twice before having to pass the ball to another player. One touch to control the ball, and the second to pass. This game helps players who run about with the ball and see nothing else.

Numbers. Each player has a number and whenever he has the ball he must play it to the next number in the sequence: 1 plays to 2, 2 plays to 3, 3 to 4 and so on.

Throw-head-catch. This game, like the others, is competitive and will improve heading ability. None of the players is allowed to run with the ball. Instead of kicking it, each player who has the ball must throw it to a team mate who has to *head* a pass. If the pass reaches its man, he in turn must *throw* it to a team mate. If the pass is intercepted by an opponent, the opponent must head a pass to one of his side. The game proceeds in this way and *only headed goals count.*

Beating a man. No player is really a good player until he can pass well and beat his man. In this game no player may pass the ball until he has beaten one opponent. This game will serve a double purpose: it will improve your passing and also your tackling at the same time.

MARKING SPACE

Using the training grid on page 11, allocate a square to each player to mark when the team has lost possession of the ball. He must deal with the opponent or opponents who come into his particular square. When possession of the ball has been won, he is free to go wherever he pleases but he will soon realise that the further he is from his own square when the ball is lost, the more running he has to do, and the more likely it is for the goal to be in danger. This particular game involves intelligent movement in relation to the other players and the ball, and will also help to create the right kind of disciplined movement.

DEFENDING AND ATTACKING FOUR GOALS

Again use can be made of the training grid with four goals, one on each side of the pitch, relating the size of the area being used to the number of players taking part. Goals can be scored in any goal. This practice is useful as it creates plenty of scoring opportunities and provides for purposeful running, emphasising all the problems that will arise in attacking and defending the goal in a real game.

MOVING OUT OF DEFENCE

Football is mainly a team game with players constantly supporting each other in attack and covering each other in defence. Defenders, however, are often apt to stand and admire their work after clearing the ball from the danger area, and thereby leaving space in front of the defence which can be exploited by the opposition as soon as they gain possession. In this game therefore, no goal will count unless the whole team scoring the goal is in the attacking half of the field.

Two-touch helps players who run about with the ball but fail to see the passing opportunities. Each player may touch the ball only twice: once to control and once to pass.

Start of play and duration

The game is divided into two equal halves of 45 minutes each for senior games, and slightly shorter halves for schoolboy games. Extra time may be allowed by the referee for injury time or other stoppages.

The choice of ends at the beginning of the match is decided by the toss of a coin (*provided by the referee*), and it is usual for the two captains to shake hands before the home captain actually tosses the coin. The captain winning the toss has the choice of ends *or* kicking off first. His decision may be based on the position of the sun or the direction of the wind.

THE RULES FOR THE KICK-OFF
The rules for kick-off are very clear:

> *1. Every player must be standing in his* own *half of the field, and players of the opposing side at least 10 yards from the ball at the moment it is kicked.*
>
> *2. The ball must roll at least the distance of its own circumference before it can be played by another player.*
>
> *3. The player taking the kick must play it forward and may not touch it again until it has been touched by another player.*
>
> *4. A goal cannot be scored direct from the kick-off.*

WHEN A GOAL IS SCORED
Once a goal has been scored the referee signals it and restarts play with a kick-off from the centre spot again, this time taken by the *non-scoring* side.

Choice of kick-off or end is decided by the toss of a coin.

Every player must be standing in his own half of the field at the moment the ball is kicked from the centre spot, and the ball must be stationary.

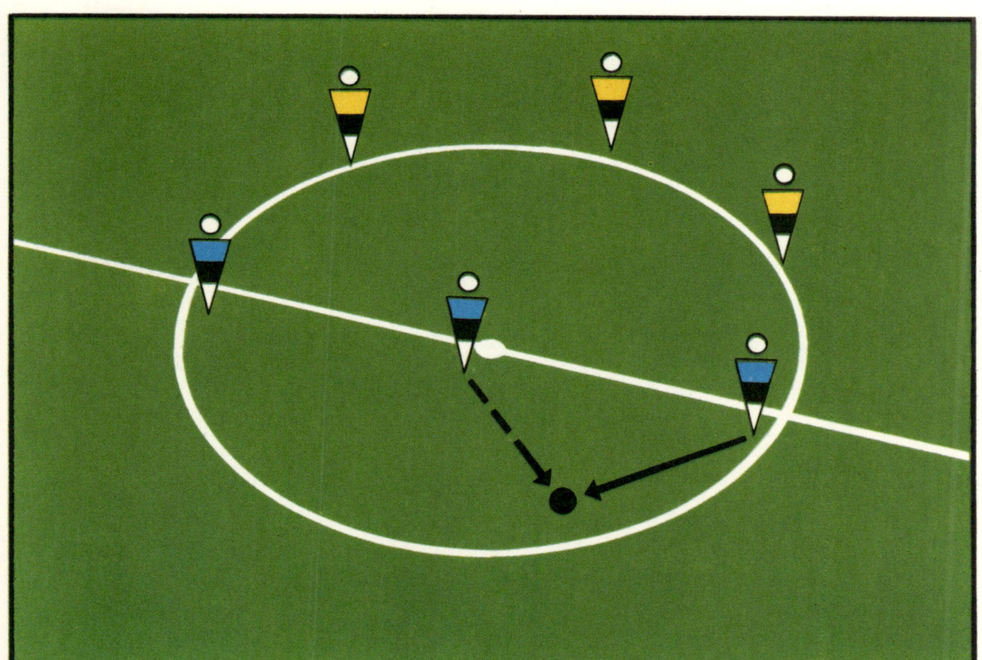

Incorrect kick-off: the player taking the kick plays the ball back instead of forward.

If the keeper saves the ball *after* the whole of it has crossed the line, the ball is *out of play*.

The ball is *out of play* only if the *whole* of it has crossed the touch line or goal-line either on the ground or in the air.

In and out of play

It is the position of the ball that determines whether it is in play or out, not the position of the players. For example, a player is not infringing any of the rules of the game if he runs *outside* the touch lines in chase of the ball so long as the ball itself remains *inside* the line.

OUT OF PLAY

The ball is *out of play* only when the *whole* of it has passed over the side line or the goal line whether it is in the air or along the ground, or when it rebounds off the goal post, crossbar or corner flag *outside* the field of play.

The ball is also out of play when the referee has stopped the game for some reason (injury, spectators on the pitch and so on).

IN PLAY

The ball is *in play* if it swerves out over the side line or the goal line and lands back in the field of play provided that in the course of its flight the *whole* of the ball does not cross the line.

It is also still in play if it rebounds off the goalpost or crossbar or corner flag *inside* the field of play.

If the ball should strike the referee or the linesmen when they are standing in the field of play, it is still in play and the game continues.

If the ball swerves out over the line in flight and finally falls in the field of play, then unless in its course the *whole* of it passed across the line, it remains *in play*.

A goal is scored when the *whole* of the ball has crossed the goal-line between the posts and below the crossbar.

Scoring

A goal is scored only when the *whole* of the ball passes over the goal line between the goal posts and under the crossbar, so long as it has not been thrown, carried or propelled by hand by one of the attacking side. If the goalkeeper catches the ball in the air before the whole of it has crossed the goal line between the posts, then a goal has *not* been scored. Similarly, if any of the defending side stops the ball on the goal line before the *whole* of it enters the goal mouth then it is *not* a goal.

The goal is *not* allowed if it is scored direct from the kick-off, a goal kick or a free kick awarded for any of the following infringements:

1. A player playing the ball a second time before it has been played by a second player at a throw-in, a free kick, a penalty kick, a corner kick, or a goal kick if the ball has passed beyond the penalty area

2. A player interfering with play when offside

3. Carrying by the goalkeeper

4. Obstruction

5. Charging the goalkeeper inside his own goal area unless he is holding the ball or obstructing an opponent

6. Ungentlemanly conduct

7. Charging an opponent at the wrong time.

After each goal is scored the players take up their positions for a place kick from the ten-yard circle, the kick being taken by the side that did *not* score.

If the keeper is still standing inside the field of play when he saves the ball but after the *whole* of it has already crossed the line in the air, then a goal has been scored.

Offside

The offside law states that a player is *offside if he is nearer to his opponent's goal-line than the ball at the moment when the ball is played* UNLESS

1. *He is in his own half of the field of play* or

2. *There are 2 opponents (one of whom may be the goalkeeper) nearer to their own goal than he is* or

3. *The ball last touched an opponent or was last played by an opponent* or

4. *He receives the ball direct from a goal kick, a corner kick, a throw-in or when it is dropped by the referee.*

THE AIM OF THE OFFSIDE RULE

The offside rule was introduced to prevent players just hanging about close to their opponent's goal, waiting for a long upfield pass and ready to shoot from close range.

The referee will only penalise an offside player if *in the referee's opinion* that player is likely to interfere with the play in any way or is seeking to gain an advantage by being offside.

The offside rule is one that many players have difficulty in understanding at first, and even more difficulty in putting into practice on the field. But because many a good chance at goal can be lost by one member of a team being caught offside, it is worth spending a little time getting to grips with this particular rule. After that, it is a matter of constantly checking your position in relation to the play to make sure that *you* are not in danger of being the offender. And if you do find yourself in an offside position, put yourself onside again as quickly as you can either by putting two defending players between you and the goal, or by getting back into your own half—whichever makes good sense in relation to the state of the play at the time. But remember that you can't put yourself back onside once the ball has been played to your advantage.

No player can be given offside if he is in his own half of the field.

If A passes to B, B is not offside *because he is in his own half*. But if A makes the pass to C, then C *is* offside because he is ahead of the ball inside his opponent's half with only the keeper between him and the goal at the moment the pass is made.

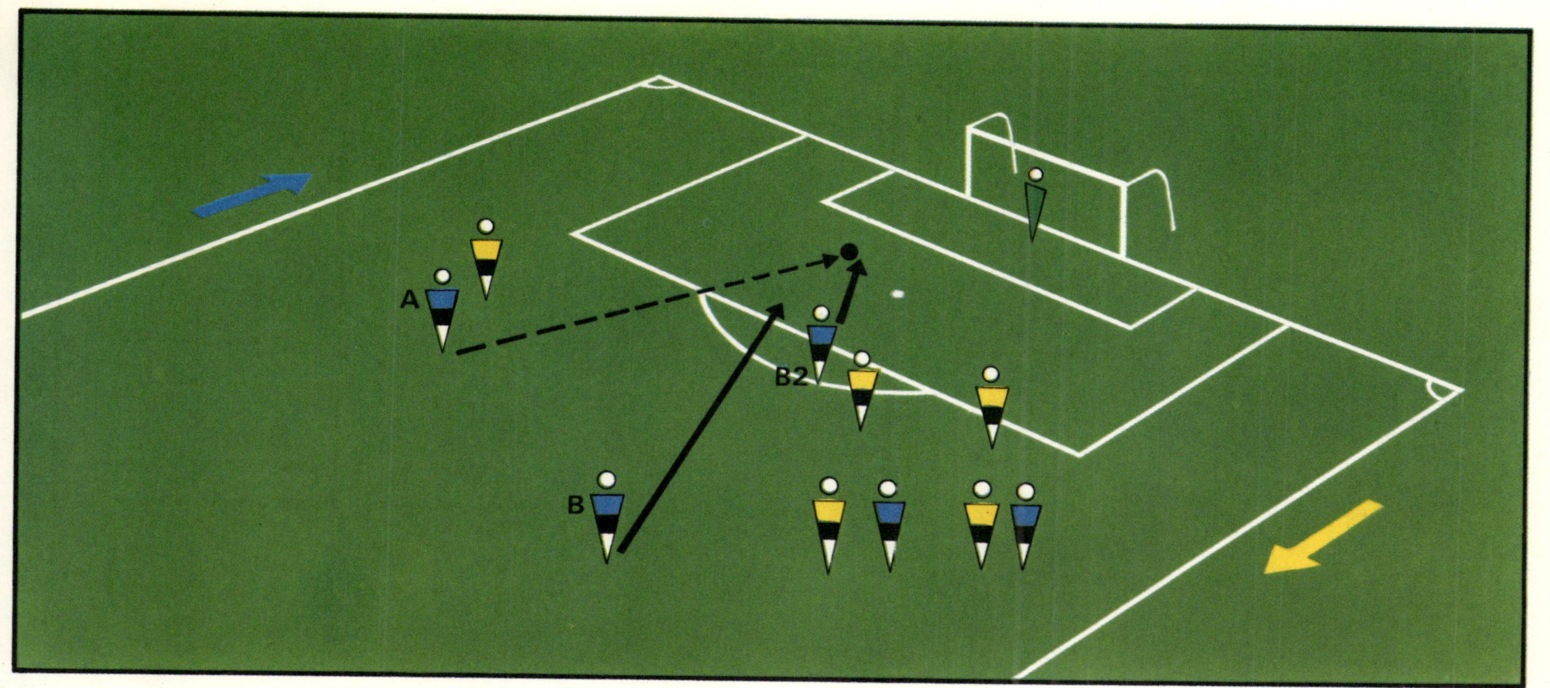

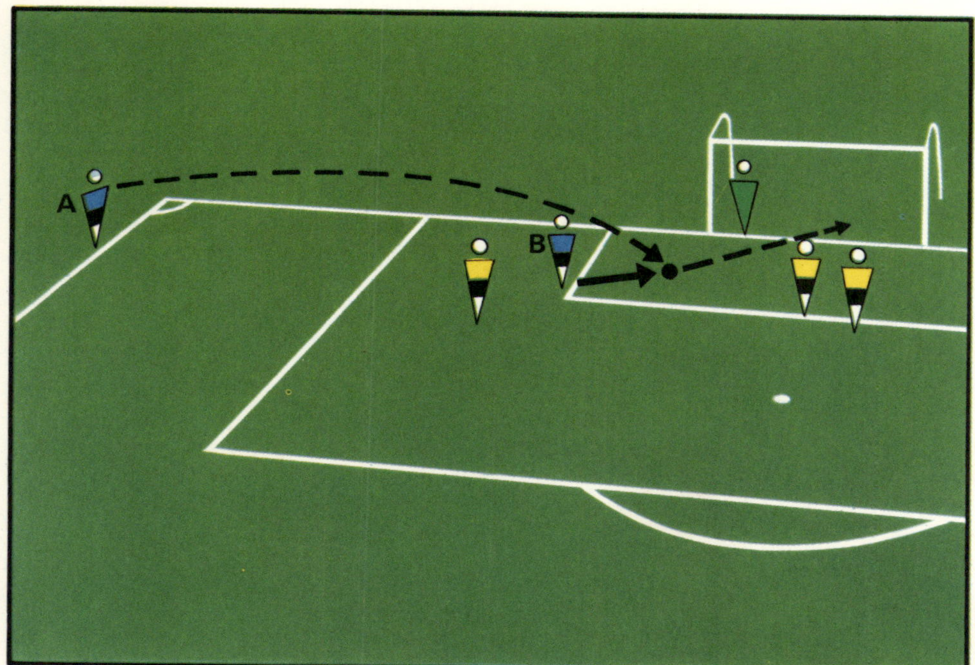

Above: if attacker A makes the pass shown by the broken line, his team mate B may run on to it without being given offside because at the moment the pass was made he was behind the ball. If, however, when the pass is made he is standing at B2, then he *is* offside because he is ahead of the ball and has only one opponent between him and the goal.

Left: although B has only the keeper between him and the goal when he takes the pass from a throw-in from A he is not offside because no player can be given offside direct from a throw-in.

If a situation arose in which attacker B received the corner pass from A and scored, the goal would be allowed. B is *not offside* because no player can be given offside direct from a corner kick.

Fouls and misconduct

The referee has the power to award free kicks to one side for offences committed by the other.

Free kicks are of two kinds: *direct* and *indirect*. They are awarded for different kinds of offence and the essential difference between them is that while a goal can be scored straight from a *direct free kick*, a goal *cannot* be scored from an *indirect free kick* unless the ball has been played by at least one other player after the player taking the kick.

DIRECT FREE KICK OFFENCES

There are nine of these and all except one are for deliberate attempts to harass or hinder opponents physically. The nine offences are:

1. Deliberately handling the ball
2. Charging an opponent dangerously
3. Charging an opponent from behind
4. Holding an opponent
5. Pushing an opponent
6. Tripping an opponent
7. Kicking or attempting to kick an opponent

Dangerous play.

Tripping.

8. Jumping at an opponent
9. Striking or attempting to strike an opponent.

INDIRECT FREE KICK OFFENCES

The following offences are penalised by an *indirect free* kick awarded to the other side:

1. Interfering with play when offside
2. Carrying by the goalkeeper
3. Obstructing an opponent
4. Dangerous play
5. Not kicking the ball forward at a penalty kick
6. Attempting to kick the ball while it is held by the goalkeeper
7. Time-wasting tactics by the keeper.

A player may also be sent off the field and barred from taking further part in the game if he is guilty of violent conduct or serious foul play if he persists in it after a warning caution from the referee. He can also be sent off for using abusive language.

Pushing and pulling.

Handling.

Obstruction.

Free kicks

DIRECT FREE KICKS WITHIN 10 YARDS OF GOAL
If a free kick is awarded against you within 10 yards of the goal, you should regard it as a serious threat. It is vital that the whole team lines up on the goal-line as quickly as possible. As soon as the ball is kicked all the players except the keeper must sprint out towards the ball in order to block the shot. All the defending players must move together so that they do not leave any gaps through which the ball may pass.

If you are on the attacking side and the players of the opposing side do not line up in this way, it is a simple matter to touch the ball to a team mate standing a couple of yards away to hammer past the startled goalkeeper. It is in fact almost as good as a penalty kick.

DIRECT FREE KICKS OUTSIDE THE PENALTY AREA
For direct free kicks awarded *outside* the penalty area, it is necessary for the offending side to set up a defensive wall to protect the goal. The wall must be made quickly, usually of two to five players who block the half of the goal nearest to the ball. The goalkeeper must also position himself quickly to cover the other half of the goal, at a point where he can see both the kicker and the ball. The keeper often assumes responsibility for lining up or 'setting' the wall. He must however be on his toes in case the kick is taken quickly.

BEATING THE WALL
The ways of trying to get the ball past the wall of defenders are numerous and they will depend on what the defending side does. As a general rule the wall can be beaten only if it is positioned badly or if the kicker can 'bend' his shot round it. Usually he has to change the shooting angle by playing the ball quickly to a team mate who has a clear sight of the goal while the players forming the wall are out of the game.

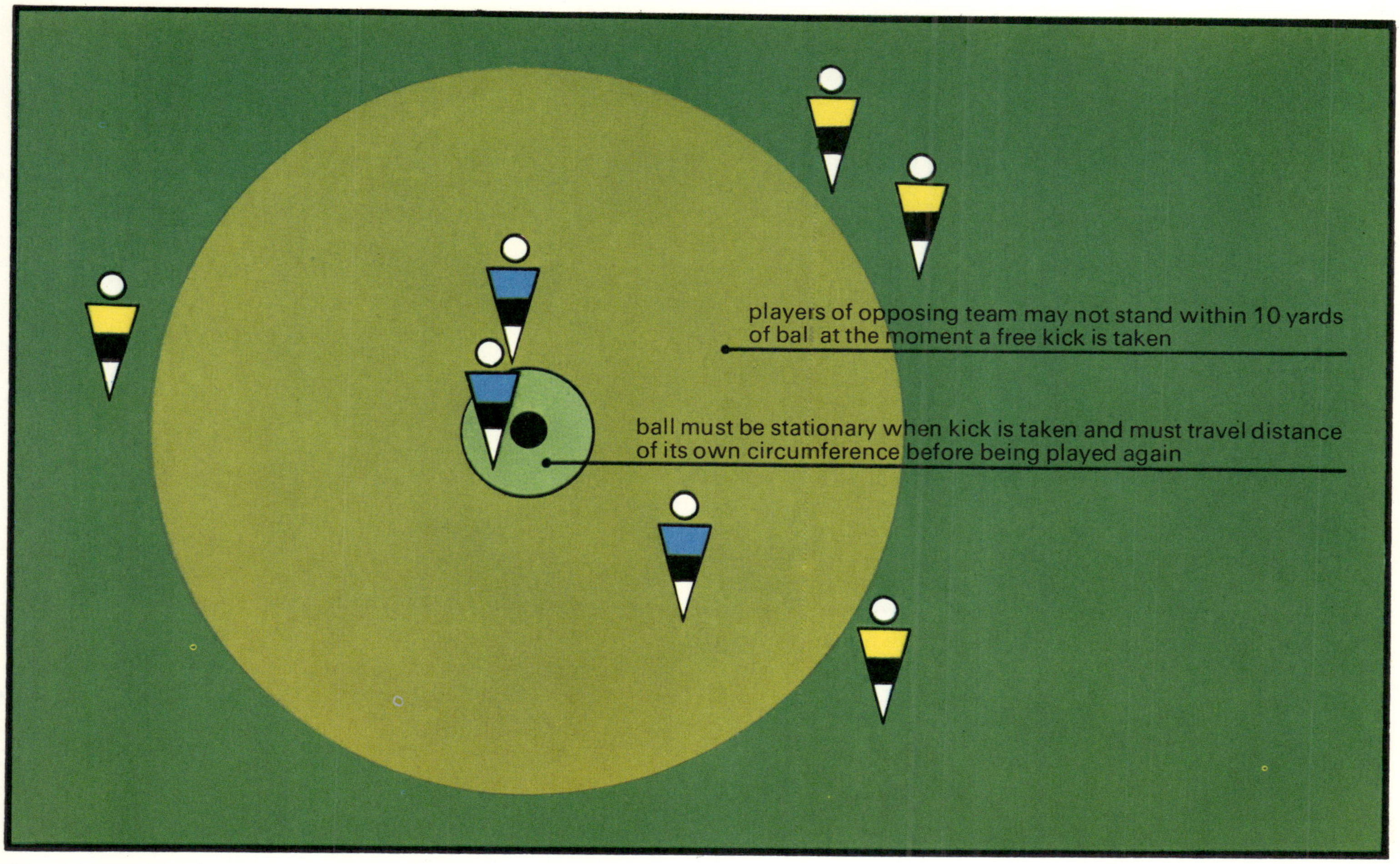

players of opposing team may not stand within 10 yards
of bal at the moment a free kick is taken

ball must be stationary when kick is taken and must travel distance
of its own circumference before being played again

Above: Opponents must stand at least ten yards away from the ball at a free kick until it is played. The ball must then travel at least the distance of its own circumference before it can be played by any other player, and the player taking the kick may not touch it again until it has been played by another player.

Below: If a free kick is given less than 10 yards from the goal the defending side may stand *on the goal-line* even if this puts them less than 10 yards from the ball.

less than 10 yards

10 yards minimum

If the keeper moves off the goal-line before the kick is taken, then it must be retaken.

Penalty kicks

If a player, *A*, from the attacking side moves forward within 10 yards of the ball before the kick is taken, the kick must be taken again.

A penalty kick is awarded for any one of the nine offences listed on page 48 if it is committed intentionally by a defending player *inside his own penalty area.* It is for the referee to decide whether the offence was deliberate or not.

The kick is taken from the penalty spot, a mark 12 yards from the goal-line and, if necessary, extra time will be added by the referee at half-time, full time and extra time to allow it to be taken properly.

TAKING THE PENALTY KICK

Opinion on the best way to take the penalty kick differs. Some players prefer to place the kick accurately just inside the post, others like to drive the ball powerfully into the net. The ball struck powerfully with the inside of the foot is more likely to be successful than the instep kick. However, *your* way is the best way for *you* if you can put the ball past the goalkeeper nine times out of ten.

It is worth watching the position taken up by the goalkeeper when you are preparing to take the kick. Often he will stand off centre, deliberately inviting you to shoot into the larger space but ready to dive in that direction immediately you strike the ball. By shooting into the area in which he is standing, you can often catch him on the wrong foot, too late to change the direction of his dive.

RULES CONTROLLING THE PENALTY KICK

1. All players except the keeper and the player taking the kick must be outside the penalty area and at least 10 yards from the ball until it is kicked.

2. The goalkeeper must stand on the goal-line without moving his feet until the ball is kicked. If the keeper moves before the kick is taken and saves the shot, the kick must be retaken.

3. The penalty kicker must play the ball forward *and cannot play it again until it has been touched by another player.*

4. The ball must travel forward the distance of its own circumference before it is in play.

5. If an attacker moves into the area before the kick is taken and a goal is scored, it does not count. The kick must be retaken.

6. If a defender *infringes any of the penalty kick rules and a goal is scored, the goal is allowed.*

7. If the ball bursts in flight, the kick is retaken.

At a penalty kick the keeper must stand on his goal-line without moving his feet until the ball is played. All other players must remain outside the penalty area and at least 10 yards from the ball.

Correct throw-in: ball held in both hands behind head, both feet on the ground behind the line.

Incorrect throw-in: one foot completely off the ground.

The throw-in

When the ball goes out of play by passing over the side line either in the air or on the ground, it is thrown in from the point where it crossed the line by an opponent of the player who last touched the ball before it went out of play.

THROW-IN RULES

1. When throwing the ball the player taking the throw must face the field of play.

2. Part of both feet must be on the ground either on the touch line or behind it but not inside the field of play.

3. The ball must be thrown with both *hands and must come from behind and over the head.*

4. A goal cannot be scored direct from a throw-in.

5. The thrower must not play the ball a second time until another player has touched it. (The penalty if he does, is an indirect free kick to the other side).

6. A player cannot be offside from a throw-in.

7. If the ball is not thrown in correctly, the game is restarted with a throw-in taken by a player of the opposing team.

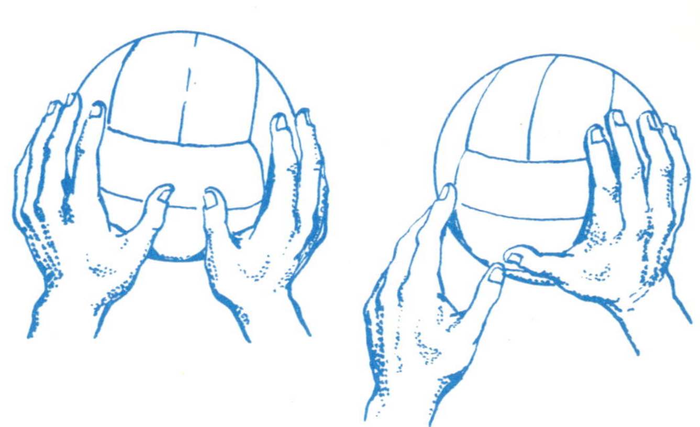

Position of hands: correct (*left*) and incorrect (*right*).

TAKING THE THROW-IN

The player taking the throw must decide which will give him the best tactical advantage: a long throw or a short throw. His choice will depend on who is least closely marked. Whatever he does he should take the throw quickly before the opposing side have time to mark his team mates. And as soon as he has thrown in he must move back into the field of play, ready to receive a pass if needed.

Incorrect throw-in: ball held above head instead of behind.

Goal kicks

A goal kick is awarded when a member of the attacking team kicks or knocks the ball over the goal-line. It is taken by a player of the defending team (usually the keeper) *from the six-yard line* on whichever side of the goal the ball crossed the goal-line or crossbar.

When a goal kick is taken it is important for the out players to create space into which the ball may be kicked, allowing one of the team to run and meet the ball, sometimes to control and attack the defending player or —if he is tightly marked—to play it off to a colleague.

The kick will go either down the middle of the field or out to the wings, but if a player on the attacking side simply stands waiting for the ball he presents no problems to his opponents and will certainly not win the ball.

RULES CONTROLLING THE GOAL KICK

1. Opponents must remain outside the penalty area *while the kick is taken.*

2. The ball is not in play until it has passed beyond the limit of the penalty area.

3. If any player other than the kicker makes contact with the ball inside the penalty area the kick must be taken again.

4. A goal cannot be scored direct from a goal kick.

5. The goalkeeper cannot receive the ball directly into his hands from a goal kick.

6. Once the ball has gone beyond the penalty area the player taking the kick may not play it again until it has been played by another player.

No time must be wasted while taking the kick.

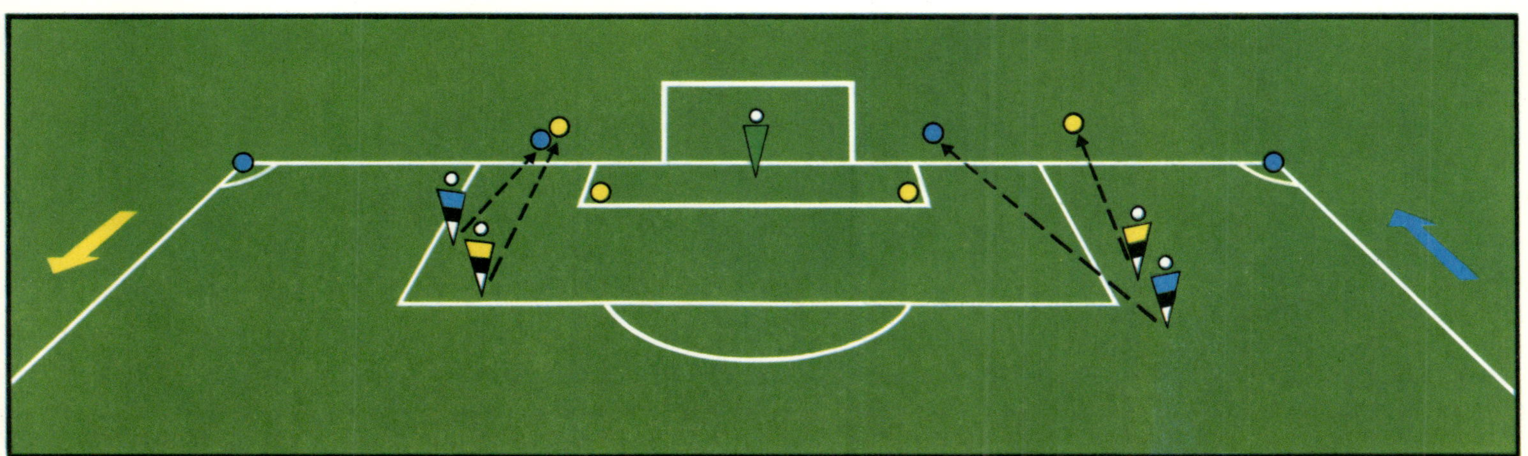

When the ball is last played by a defender before crossing the goal line a *corner kick* is given to the attacking side. When the ball is last played by an attacker before going out over the goal line, a goal kick is given to the defenders. Both the corner kick and the goal kick are taken on the side of the goal on which the ball went out of play.

Corner kicks

A corner kick is awarded when the ball passes over the goal-line having been played *last* by a *defending* player. The kick is taken by a player from the *attacking* side from the corner nearest to the point where the ball went out of play.

Goals from corner kicks are difficult to bring off but by following set patterns of play that have been well rehearsed in training, you can deceive the defenders and earn a rich reward for hard work.

MAKING THE MOST OF A CORNER

The first thing for the attackers to do is to ensure that the kick isn't wasted. All too often the ball goes behind the goal for a goal kick to the defending side. The player who takes the corner must have the ability to reach the target area and he must also avoid the goalkeeper, either by dropping the ball short or by playing it beyond the keeper.

For the goalkeeper it is without doubt the inswinging corner kick that presents the greatest hazard, especially as he has one eye on the ball and the other on the eager striker who comes leaping in with a powerfully headed shot. His best position for a corner is on the goal-line by the far post, ready to move across if necessary.

The advantage at a corner lies with the forward running in to meet the ball, for the defenders have two jobs to keep them busy: the first is to mark the attackers, and the second is to watch the ball. The timing of the run to meet the ball is important. Run too soon and you advertise your plan to the other side. Run too late and you will probably see the ball being kicked downfield by the defence.

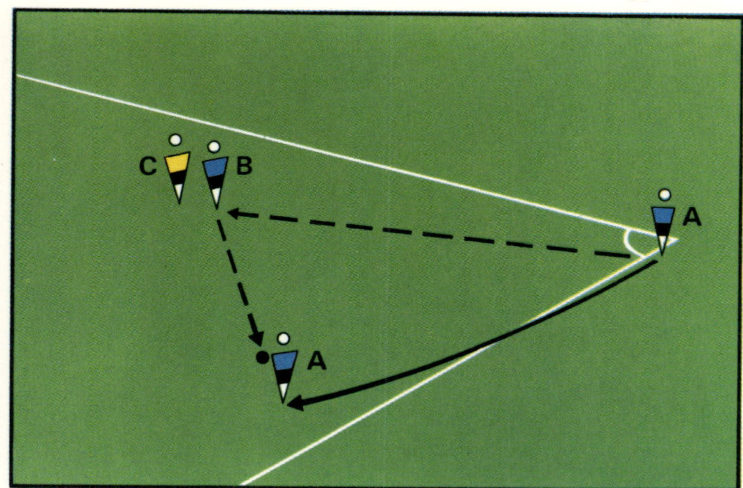

Left: at a short corner the taker of the kick, A, moves quickly into the field of play to take a pass from B.

Below: attacker B heads a high corner kick from A downwards into the path of oncoming team mate C who has sprinted in to take a shot at goal.

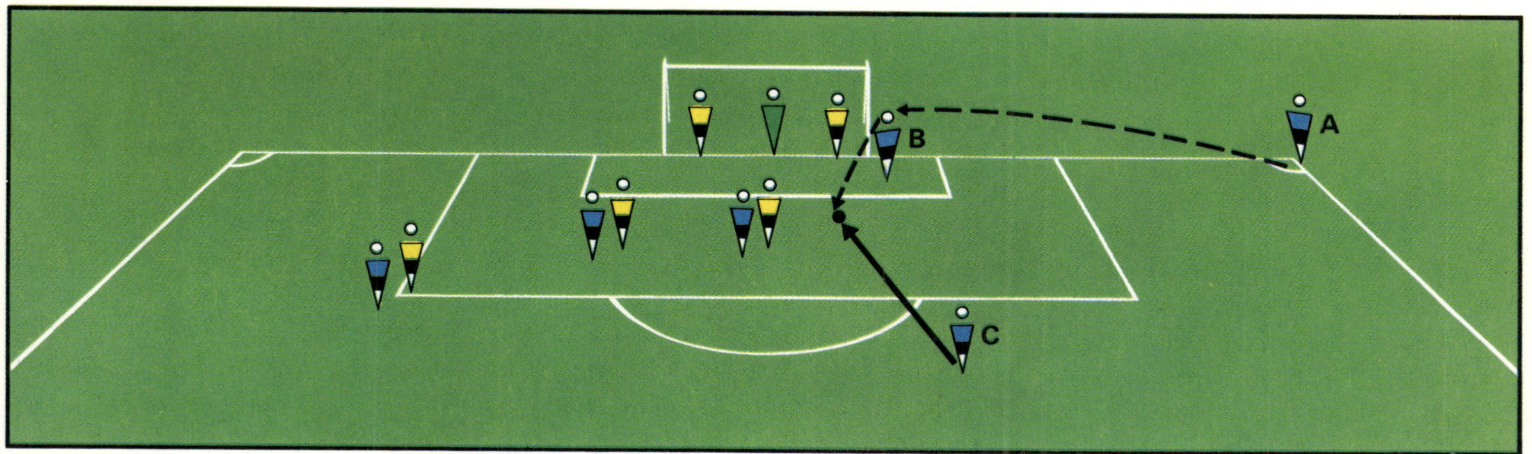

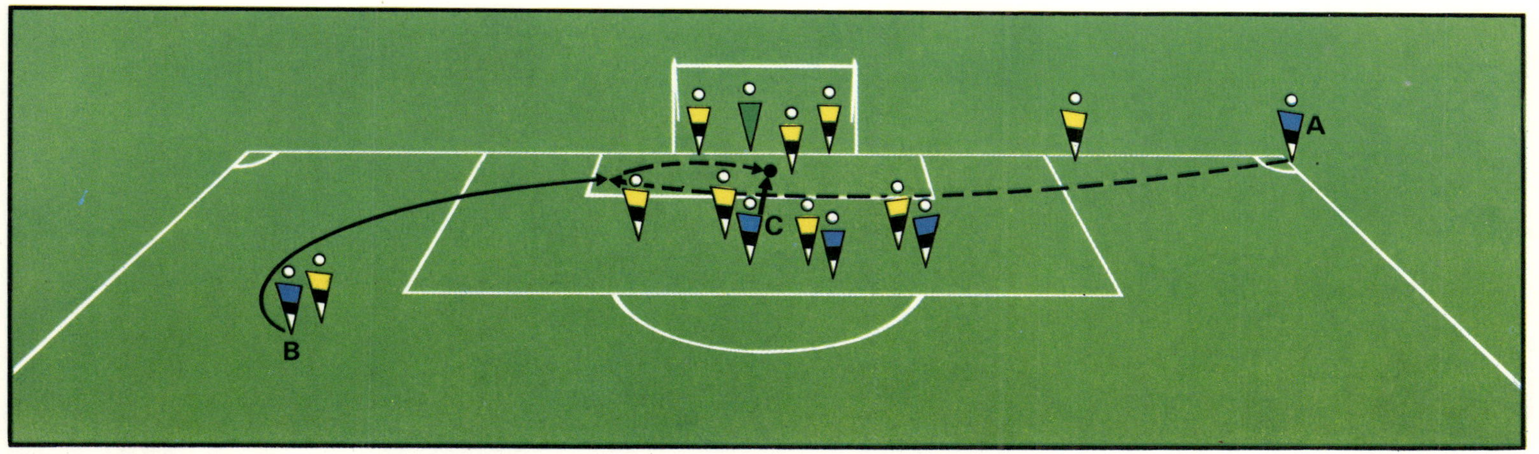

Attacking from a corner kick can swing the play from one side of the field to the other. Here attacker A sends the ball across to the far side of the goal. B evades his marker and runs in to head the ball down to the feet of team mate C directly in front of the goal.

POSITION OF THE KEEPER AT A CORNER KICK

He must be on his toes and in a position to see both the kicker and the ball. He must also be alive to the fact that the inswinging kick can creep into the net just inside the near post.

As the goalkeeper is the only player allowed to use his hands it is reasonable to assume that he will deal with any ball in the air which comes into the six-yard area. Defending players will expect him to take charge in this way.

Once again the goalkeeper must keep his eye on the flight of the ball and not be influenced too much by the movement of players in front of him.

The three basic corner kicks (the inswinger, out-swinger and short kick) can pose different problems for the keeper. He must learn to deal with them all.

CORNER KICK RULES

1. A goal may be scored direct from a corner kick.

2. The ball must be placed inside the corner circle at the corner flag before it is kicked.

3. The corner flag must not be moved when the kick is taken.

4. Opposing players must not approach within 10 yards until the ball has travelled the distance of its own circumference.

5. The player taking the corner must not touch the ball again until it has been played by another player (either of his own side or one of his opponents).

Your decision

A good team player needs a thorough knowledge of the rules of the game. The illustrations on this page depict only a few examples of the situations you may encounter on the field. Do you know the correct decision in each case?

A player runs outside the touch line in chase of the ball. Is this allowed?

Yes, so long as the ball itself remains inside the field of play. It is the position of the ball not the player that determines whether the ball is in play or not.

The player taking the throw-in follows up quickly and immediately plays the ball again to a team mate. Is this allowed?

An indirect free kick should be taken by a player from the opposing side from the point at which the infringement occurred.

At kick-off one of the players from the team not taking the kick moves inside the centre circle before the ball has been played. What is the penalty for his infringement of the rules?

There is no penalty but the kick must be retaken.

At kick-off the player taking the kick boots the ball straight into goal. Has he scored?

No. The rules state that a goal cannot be scored direct from a kick-off.

The keeper takes 5 steps without releasing the ball. What is the correct decision?

The keeper may not take more than 4 steps without releasing the ball. An indirect kick is awarded to the other side.

A ball aimed at the goal by an attacker hits the referee and rebounds into the goal. Is the goal allowed?

Yes.

Championship records

OLYMPIC WINNERS

1908	United Kingdom
1912	United Kingdom
1920	Belgium
1924	Uruguay
1928	Uruguay
1936	Italy
1948	Sweden
1952	Hungary
1956	Russia
1960	Yugoslavia
1964	Hungary
1968	Hungary
1972	Poland

WORLD CUP

1930	Uruguay
1934	Italy
1938	Italy
1950	Uruguay
1954	Germany
1958	Brazil
1962	Brazil
1966	England
1970	Brazil
1974	....

EUROPEAN CUP

1956	Real Madrid
1957	Real Madrid
1958	Real Madrid
1959	Real Madrid
1960	Real Madrid
1961	Benfica
1962	Benfica
1963	A.C. Milan
1964	Inter-Milan
1965	Inter-Milan
1966	Real Madrid
1967	Glasgow Celtic
1968	Manchester United
1969	A.C. Milan
1970	Feyenoord
1971	Ajax Amsterdam
1972	Ajax Amsterdam
1973	....
1974	....

EUROPEAN CUP WINNERS CUP

1961	A.C.Fiorentina
1962	Atletico Madrid
1963	Tottenham Hotspur
1964	Sporting Club, Lisbon
1965	West Ham United
1966	Borussia Dortmund
1967	Bayern Munich
1968	A.C. Milan
1969	Slovan Bratislava
1970	Manchester City
1971	Chelsea
1972	Glasgow Rangers
1973	....
1974	....

EUROPEAN FAIRS CUP (E.U.F.A.)

1955-58	Barcelona
1958-60	Barcelona
1960-61	A.S. Roma
1961-62	Valencia
1962-63	Valencia
1963-64	Real Zaragoza
1964-65	Ferencvaros
1965-66	Barcelona
1966-67	Dynamo Zagreb
1967-68	Leeds United
1968-69	Newcastle United
1969-70	Arsenal
1970-71	Leeds United
1971-72	Tottenham Hotspur
1972-73	....
1973-74	....

F.A. CUP WINNERS

1872	Wanderers
1873	Wanderers
1874	Oxford University
1875	Royal Engineers
1876	Wanderers
1877	Wanderers
1878	Wanderers
1879	Old Etonians
1880	Clapham R.
1881	Old Carthusians
1882	Old Etonians
1883	Blackburn Olympic
1884	Blackburn Rovers
1885	Blackburn Rovers
1886	Blackburn Rovers
1887	Aston Villa
1888	W.B.A.
1889	Preston N.E.
1890	Blackburn Rovers
1891	Blackburn Rovers
1892	W.B.A.
1893	Wolverhampton W.
1894	Notts. Co.
1895	Aston Villa
1896	Sheffield W.
1897	Aston Villa
1898	Nottingham F.
1899	Sheffield U.
1900	Bury
1901	Tottenham H.
1902	Sheffield U.
1903	Bury
1904	Manchester C.
1905	Aston Villa
1906	Everton
1907	Sheffield W.
1908	Wolverhampton W.
1909	Manchester United
1910	Newcastle United
1911	Bradford C.
1912	Barnsley
1913	Aston Villa
1914	Burnley
1915	Sheffield U.
1920	Aston Villa
1921	Tottenham H.
1922	Huddersfield
1923	Bolton W.
1924	Newcastle United
1925	Sheffield U.
1926	Bolton W.
1927	Cardiff C.
1928	Blackburn Rovers
1929	Bolton W.
1930	Arsenal
1931	W.B.A.
1932	Newcastle United
1933	Everton
1934	Manchester C.
1935	Sheffield W.
1936	Arsenal
1937	Sunderland
1938	Preston N.E.
1939	Portsmouth
1946	Derby Co.
1947	Charlton Ath.
1948	Manchester U.
1949	Wolverhampton W.
1950	Arsenal
1951	Newcastle United
1952	Newcastle United
1953	Blackpool
1954	W.B.A.
1955	Newcastle United
1956	Manchester C.
1957	Aston Villa
1958	Bolton W.
1959	Nottingham F.
1960	Wolverhampton W.
1961	Tottenham H.
1962	Tottenham H.
1963	Manchester U.
1964	West Ham U.
1965	Liverpool
1966	Everton
1967	Tottenham H.
1968	W.B.A.
1969	Manchester C.
1970	Chelsea
1971	Arsenal
1972	Leeds United
1973	....

WORLD CLUB CHAMPIONSHIP

1960	Real Madrid
1961	Penarol (Uruguay)
1962	Santos
1963	Santos
1964	Inter-Milan
1965	Inter-Milan
1966	Penarol
1967	Racing, Argentina
1968	Estudiantes (Argentina)
1969	A.C. Milan
1970	Feyenoord (Holland)
1971	Nacional (Uruguay)
1972	Ajax, Amsterdam
1973	....

FOOTBALL LEAGUE CUP

1960-61	Aston Villa
1961-62	Norwich City
1962-63	Birmingham City
1963-64	Leicester City
1964-65	Chelsea
1965-66	West Bromwich Albion
1966-67	Queen's Park Rangers
1967-68	Leeds United
1968-69	Swindon Town
1969-70	Manchester City
1970-71	Tottenham Hotspur
1971-72	Stoke City
1972-73	....
1973-74	....